RELEASING VISION

THE POWER TO CHANGE YOUR DESTINY

BISHOP SENYO BULLA

Releasing Vision

Copyright ©2021 Bishop Senyo Bulla

All rights reserved. No part of this publication may be reproduced, distributed or transmitted in any form or by any means, including photocopying, recording, or other electronic or mechanical methods, without the prior written permission of the publisher, except in the case of brief quotations embodied in critical reviews and certain other noncommercial uses permitted by copyright law.

Unless otherwise indicated, Scriptures are taken from the KING JAMES VERSION (KJV), public domain.

Scripture quotations followed by AMPC are taken from The Amplified® Bible, Copyright © 1954, 1958, 1962, 1964, 1965, 1987, by the Lockman Foundation. Used by permission. (www.Lockman.org.) All rights reserved.

Published by: HigherLife Publishing & Marketing
 PO Box 623307
 Oviedo, FL 32762
 AHigherLife.com

ISBN: 978-1-954533-63-9 (Paperback)
ISBN: 978-1-954533-64-6 (Ebook)

Printed in the United States of America.

10 9 8 7 6 5 4 3 2 1

DEDICATION

To all who are believing God for revival in their generation.

To all who are desperately crying out
for a move of God in their generation.

More prayer. Keep praying. Don't stop praying. More prayer.

God richly bless you for your labor of love.

TABLE OF CONTENTS

Foreword vii

Introduction vii

Chapter 1: The Realm of Vision 1

Chapter 2: Vision or Ambition 9

Chapter 3. The Fatal Consequences of Ambition 17

Chapter 4: Generational Blessings: The Product of Vision 29

Chapter 5: The Plans and Purposes of God 39

Chapter 6: The Crisis 45

Chapter 7: Supernatural Transportation 53

Chapter 8: Prophesy 71

FOREWORD

If you don't know where you're going, how will you know if you get there?

You've likely heard this phrase before. The truth is that you and I are on a journey through life—and we only get one pass! There are no do-overs, no repeats. So it makes sense that we be intentional in living each day of our lives with the most vision and sense of mission possible.

One of the many things I love about Bishop Bulla is his commitment to envisioning, encouraging, and empowering people to live their lives on course, on mission, to pursue a God-given spiritual and financial destiny. This is what the two messages you have in your hands is all about, equipping you to discern the divine path God has for your life.

Sadly, many people spend much of their life moving through it rather aimlessly, with little or no thought to any destinations along the way. They wander. But wandering is never what God plans for us. Consider the children of Israel ... their intention was to leave Egypt and set a course straight for the promised land. That journey could have taken less than two weeks. But because of their sin, their lack of belief and faith, they were sentenced to wander. They wandered in the wilderness for forty years before entering their promised land. Wandering through life, though, is never God's best for you. It's not God's design for you. Oh sure, He will allow you to wander if that is your intent. But wandering through life is not what God intends for you.

On the contrary, God wants to give you a path to follow, a course to pursue. God wants you to embrace and step into your destiny! These two messages are all about just that. They are all about helping you discover, embrace, pursue, and accomplish your destiny, the divine plan God has marked out for you.

Releasing Vision — The power to change your destiny is a wonderful resource to help you discover your spiritual desti- ny. Your life will have more meaning, more significance, purpose, and joy when you live it according to the divine destiny God has prepared for you. But how can you live according to your destiny if you don't know it? ***Releasing Vision*** will guide you onto the purposeful path of promise that God has for you. The Bible makes it clear that without vision the people perish (Prov. 29:18). You need to know God's vision for your life to release it.

In a similar way, ***Kingdom Wealth — Keys to accessing your financial destiny*** is a message that will compel you to be more intentional in building a financial path to promise and prosperity. Does God want you to be rich? I submit that what God wants is for you to be *fruitful*. He wants you to have the means to live generously without hinderances blocking your pursuit of the things He wants you to accomplish. When you invest your time, your money, and your life in the things God has called you to do, you will truly be rich. Does that mean you will have a fat bank account? Maybe. But the goal is not money. Remember Jesus's words when He said you can't serve God and money. God does not want you to be a slave to your finances. He wants you to master them.

I encourage you to read both of these powerful messages and ask the Holy Spirit to write on your heart and mind the things He wants you to learn. Then be intentional in pursuing the Kingdom and financial destiny He has for you.

David W. Welday III
President, HigherLife Publishing and Marketing

INTRODUCTION

It is such a great delight to welcome you into a new apostolic and prophetic season; one filled with great excitement because the supernatural power of God is about to do the remarkable. This is a strategic moment on God's prophetic calendar, and I know without a shadow of doubt He is bringing you into divine encounters. Encounters that will supernaturally position you for new heights of destiny!

Beloved, a fresh breath of the Holy Spirit is blowing across the nations. This powerful presence of God is bringing all things into alignment for the fulfillment of the purposes of God for these end times. His plans and purposes include those He has for you and your loved ones.

This is a season to press deeper into God for new divine encounters that become the foundation of new divine assignments and exploits. This is a season of accelerated momentum that will catalyze and bring about the release of multiple breakthroughs.

It is said that focus produces concentration and concentration produces acceleration and acceleration produces momentum which results in breakthroughs. You must stay focused as you read on to obtain all the blessings that God has for you in this exciting, illuminating, and life-transforming experience.

The revelation of *Releasing Vision: The Power to Change Your Destiny* is a crucial and important adventure of discovery. The adventure you are about to embark on at this strategic moment in your life will supernaturally position you for greatness. The events unraveling in this generation and the generations to come require new dimensions of revelation for new dimensions of spiritual warfare.

God has great and tremendous plans for you. However, the enemy by constantly changing and upgrading his arsenal, also has plans for you. It is time for you to destroy all the fatal consequences of ambition and come into the generational blessings produced by vision. Remember, "Where there is no vision, the people perish" (Prov. 29:18). This is your season to access the unfolding of the mystery of vision.

CHAPTER ONE

THE REALM OF VISION

There is a natural or physical realm governed by the five senses and there is a supernatural or spiritual realm governed by faith.

> *Now faith is the substance of things hoped for, the evidence of things not seen. For by it the elders obtained a good report. Through faith we understand that the worlds were framed by the word of God, so that things which are seen were not made of things which do appear.*
> —Hebrews 11:1-3

We see in this scripture that there are things seen, which are natural and exist in the physical realm, and there are things unseen, which are supernatural and exist in the spiritual realm.

Vision deals with the sense of sight and it is important for you to understand different kinds of sight, especially spiritual sight.

- Foresight deals with imaginations of future events.
- Hindsight deals with memories and past events.

- Insight deals with a clear understanding of the true nature of things.

- Spiritual sight goes beyond the natural or physical realm into the events of the supernatural and spiritual realm.

- Dreams and visions reveal the plans and purposes of God or Satan.

> *For God speaketh once, yea twice, yet man perceiveth it not. In a dream, in a vision of the night, when deep sleep falleth upon men, in slumberings upon the bed; Then he openeth the ears of men, and sealeth their instruction.*
>
> —Job 33:14-16

Dreams and visions are one way God communicates His plans and purposes to man. God is a supernatural being who lives in a realm far beyond human conception, and from that realm, He carries out His operations.

God created the world, and He has plans and purposes for His creation.

> *In the beginning God created the heaven and the earth. And the earth was without form, and void; and darkness was upon the face of the deep. And the Spirit of God moved upon the face of the waters. And God said, Let there be light: and there was light.*
>
> —Genesis 1:1-3

> *And God said, Let us make man in our image, after our likeness: and let them have dominion over the fish of the sea,*

and over the fowl of the air, and over the cattle, and over all the earth, and over every creeping thing that creepeth upon the earth. So God created man in his own image, in the image of God created he him; male and female created he them. And God blessed them, and God said unto them, Be fruitful, and multiply, and replenish the earth, and subdue it: and have dominion over the fish of the sea, and over the fowl of the air, and over every living thing that moveth upon the earth.

—Genesis 1:26-28

God created you, and He has plans and purposes for you that He communicates to you through spiritual sight. His plans and purposes are known as the counsel of God. The Trinity made up of the Father, the Son and the Holy Spirit sit in counsel and when ready, they step out of the supernatural or spiritual realm into the natural or physical realm to execute their plans. Thus, Godly dreams and visions are of the spiritual realm and are the counsel of God.

God created man is His own image and gave them dominion over the earth. God did not leave man alone in the Garden of Eden. He provided Godly counsel, counsel He continues to provide His children today because of the life, death, and resurrection of Jesus Christ. The counsel of God is the most important thing you must be concerned about in every season of your life, because God's counsel involves the plans and purposes of God from generation to generation.

The Lord bringeth the counsel of the heathen to nought: he maketh the devices of the people of none effect. The counsel of the Lord standeth for ever, the thoughts of his heart to all generations.

—Psalm 33:10-11

The counsel of God are events the Most High has conceived in His thoughts and dreams that He has determined to accomplish and execute.

The Lord of hosts hath sworn, saying, Surely as I have thought, so shall it come to pass; and as I have purposed, so shall it stand.... For the Lord of hosts hath purposed, and who shall disannul it? and his hand is stretched out, and who shall turn it back?

— Isaiah 14:24, 27

These God-purposed events are not suggestions that are up for discussion. These are divine purposes that will come to pass, and out of divine prerogative He chooses to reveal them to whomever He chooses. You should count yourself highly favored when you are chosen by the sovereignty of God to receive these divine communications, which in effect, bring you into realms of divine assignments.

Vision exists in a realm where God dwells and operates and executes His counsel and purposes. In order for you to access the realm of vision and understand the mysteries of vision, you must be willing to see the invisible.

By faith he forsook Egypt, not fearing the wrath of the king: for he endured, as seeing him who is invisible.

—Hebrews 11:27

The Realm of Vision

When you see the invisible, you can do the impossible! As a child of God, you have access to God's counsel, you can see the invisible and accomplish the impossible. Don't worry, doubt, or fear you are not alone in this endeavor.

Moses had divine encounters with the invisible God through the burning bush experience, which was the beginning of his supernatural training in bringing about God's awesome signs and wonders.

> *Now Moses kept the flock of Jethro his father-in-law, the priest of Midian: and he led the flock to the backside of the desert, and came to the mountain of God, even to Horeb. And the angel of the Lord appeared unto him in a flame of fire out of the midst of a bush: and he looked, and, behold, the bush burned with fire, and the bush was not consumed. And Moses said, I will now turn aside, and see this great sight, why the bush is not burnt. And when the Lord saw that he turned aside to see, God called unto him out of the midst of the bush and said, Moses, Moses. And he said, Draw not nigh hither: put off thy shoes from off thy feet, for the place whereon thou standest is holy ground.*
>
> —Exodus 3:1-5

Now, the ability to see the invisible does not make sense in the natural, in the place where our five senses dominate. It does not make sense because to see the invisible you have to step out of the realm of the five senses and into the realm of faith. Everything about the realm of vision operates and functions under the laws of faith. If you are unwilling to operate under the laws of faith, you will not be able to access the realm of vision.

You might be asking, *How do I see the invisible or Him who is invisible?*

As you embark on this adventure of discovery, you will begin to understand how to access God's counsel. This is your goal and to accomplish it your focus must be on seeing the invisible. This means your focus is not going to be on natural sight, but on supernatural sight. When you come into supernatural sight, you will see what others cannot see.

When you see the invisible, you access the realm of vision, you will discover your purpose, assignment, calling, ministry, mission, and destiny. That is the reason for the scripture verse "Where there is no vision, the people perish" (Prov. 29:18a).

"People perish" this context means:

- The people are idle or they play. They cast off all restraint and discipline for lack of instruction and clear direction. They live in a state of carelessness and recklessness.

- The people are scattered. They have no focus or concentration. They are like sheep without a shepherd. To be without a prophetic word is a terrible state or condition to live in. You will be confused and all over the place without any purpose or direction.

- The people rebel. Where there is no revelation, people live in a state of apostasy. They are lawless and do whatever they want to do. They are in a state of turbulence and they despise God's dominion. They rebel against God and His delegated authority and see nothing wrong with it. This is the foundation of witchcraft.

- The people are naked. All the above activities leave people in spiritual, physical, moral, mental, psychological, emotional, relational, and financial poverty and bankruptcy.
- The people are destroyed. The lack of knowledge, especially spiritual knowledge, understanding, and wisdom leads to destruction.

These truths are rooted in Scripture.

My people are destroyed for lack of knowledge: because thou hast rejected knowledge, I will also reject thee, that thou shalt be no priest to me: seeing thou hast forgotten the law of thy God, I will also forget thy children.

—Hosea 4:6

Therefore my people are gone into captivity, because they have no knowledge: and their honourable men are famished, and their multitude dried up with thirst

—Isaiah 5:13

It is time for you to aggressively make your way into the realm of vision in order to escape the consequences of a life without a vision or purpose.

God is a Spirit: and they that worship him must worship him in spirit and in truth.

—John 4:24

Remember, you do not see the invisible until you come into a particular realm, the realm of the supernatural. That is where God lives and where He operates.

Then the word of the Lord came unto me, saying, Before I formed thee in the belly I knew thee; and before thou camest forth out of the womb I sanctified thee, and I ordained thee a prophet to the nations.

—Jeremiah 1:4-5

For I know the thoughts that I think toward you, saith the Lord, thoughts of peace, and not of evil, to give you an expected end. Then shall ye call upon me, and ye shall go and pray unto me, and I will hearken unto you. And ye shall seek me, and find me, when ye shall search for me with all your heart. And I will be found of you, saith the Lord.

—Jeremiah 29:11-14a

God has a plan and purpose for your life. His counsel concerning your life is waiting for you. It is time for you to discover and fulfill the counsel of God for your life.

CHAPTER TWO

VISION OR AMBITION

There is a very strong difference between a God-given vision and a personal ambition. A vision is the unfolding of God's plans and purposes, or the counsel of God, to an individual. This is usually accomplished through one form of divine revelation or another.

Remember, God is a Spirit, and He lives and operates from the supernatural, the spiritual realm. When God wants to communicate His plans and purposes, He does that by stepping out of the realm of the supernatural into the realm of the natural and by revelation. He communicates His plans to whomever He wants.

What is man, that thou art mindful of him? and the Son of man, that thou visitest him? For thou hast made him a little lower than the angels, and hast crowned him with glory and honor. Thou madest him to have dominion over the works of thy hands; thou has put all things under his feet.

—Psalm 8:4-6

It is important for you to understand that a vision is obtained through the visitations of God. It is obtained through divine encounters when God reveals Himself to you. You cannot receive a vision without a divine encounter.

A vision from God's counsel is spiritual and supernatural whilst ambitions are carnal, which is fleshly or natural. There is an immense difference between that which is spiritual and that which is carnal or fleshly. When something is carnal or fleshly, it originates from the imagination of man. It comes out of egoistic activities and it is full of pride and vain glory. It does not originate from God.

The main difference between a God-given vision and a personal ambition is the source or origin. If the source is divine, or from God, then it is vision. If the source is human or from natural agendas or plans then it is ambition. It does not matter how good or beautiful a thing looks; if it is not from God, then it is ambition. There is a vast difference between good plans and God plans.

Good plans originate from man and God plans or the plans and purposes of God originate from God. Please do not deceive yourself, honesty and humility are very important when it comes to the issues of vision because you are dealing with God who is a Spirit.

The unfolding of the mystery of vision is a tremendous blessing to those who have chosen the path of the supernatural or spiritual. Before you give your life to Christ, you are described by the scriptures as a natural man. According to the scriptures, the natural man cannot receive the teachings and revelation of the Spirit of God because they are foolishness to him.

> *But the natural, non-spiritual man does not accept or welcome or admit into his heart the gifts and teachings and revelations of the Spirit of God, for they are folly (meaningless, nonsense) to him; and he is incapable of knowing them (of progressively recognizing, understanding, and becoming better acquainted with them) because they are spiritually discerned and estimated and appreciated.*
> —1 Corinthians 2:14 AMPC

Even after you give your life to Christ and become a child of God, if you do not humble yourself and renew your mind, you still cannot receive the teachings and revelation of the Spirit of God because you have a carnal mind and you are described by the scriptures as a carnal man.

> *For they that are after the flesh do mind the things of the flesh; but they that are after the Spirit the things of the Spirit. For to be carnally minded is death; but to be spiritually minded is life and peace. Because the carnal mind is enmity against God: for it is not subject to the law of God, neither indeed can be. So then they that are in the flesh cannot please God.*
> —Romans 8:5-8

The carnal mind is the unrenewed and unregenerated mind. You have to understand that man is a tripartite being. Meaning he is in three dimensions spirit, soul and body. The spirit of man is the portion of his being that is regenerated or born again and the Holy Spirit comes to dwell in the spirit of man.

The fact that your spirit is regenerated does not mean that your mind is also regenerated. It is your responsibility to renew your mind. God will not do that for you. This is the challenge for most of God's people. You are born again, Spirit-filled, tongue-talking, booked and confirmed for heaven, but you have an unregenerated and unrenewed mind.

> *I beseech you therefore brethren, by the mercies of God, that ye present your bodies a living sacrifice, holy, acceptable unto God, which is your reasonable service. And be not conformed to this world: but be ye transformed by the renewing of your mind, that ye may prove what is that good, and acceptable, and perfect, will of God.*
>
> —Romans 12:1-2

The renewing of your mind is pivotal to your spiritual growth:

- It determines whether you will come into the realm of vision or not.
- It determines whether you will grow in faith or not.
- It determines whether you will be able to overcome the enemy or not.
- It determines whether you will be able to possess the promises of God or not.

- It determines whether you will be a spiritual Christian or a carnal Christian.

- It determines whether you will operate in the realm of vision or ambition.

- It determines everything about your life and prophetic destiny.

The issues of the renewed mind are serious. They are life or death in nature.

- The unregenerated or unrenewed mind is an enemy of God. It is a major tool and instrument in the hands of the enemy to fight and oppose you.

- The unrenewed or the carnal mind is a lethal weapon in the hands of the enemy that causes you to self-destruct and abort your prophetic destiny.

- The unrenewed or carnal mind cannot submit to the laws, teachings, and revelation of God, His Word, and His Spirit.

- The unrenewed or carnal mind is the source of rebellion against God, His Word, the Holy Spirit, and God's delegated authority.

- The unrenewed or carnal mind is the foundation for witchcraft on all levels and in every dimension. It is the foundation for all platforms of witchcraft.

> *But they rebelled, and vexed his Holy Spirit: therefore he was turned to be their enemy, and he fought against them.*
>
> —Isaiah 63:10

The fact that you have a title: child of God, minister, deacon, elder, pastor, or any other business, executive, or political title does not mean that God's Holy Spirit will not fight you! If you continue to maintain the unrenewed or carnal mind, you have positioned yourself to be an enemy of God and His plans and purposes, and He will aggressively fight and destroy you!

God will fight you because you are operating in rebellion and witchcraft. The unrenewed and carnal mind is the foundation of rebellion, stubbornness, passive aggressiveness, and witchcraft in the church.

Today, you must choose to be either a spiritual Christian or a carnal Christian. Choosing to be a carnal Christian is dangerous and detrimental to your destiny. The carnal Christian with the unrenewed and unregenerated mind is a carrier of many demons and disembodied personalities. The demons and disembodied personalities dwell in, lodge, and inhabit the carnal mind.

> *For those who are according to the flesh and are controlled by its unholy desires set their minds on and pursue those things which gratify the flesh, but those who are according to the Spirit and are controlled by the desires of the Spirit set their minds on and seek those things which gratify the [Holy] Spirit.*
>
> *Now the mind of the flesh [which is sense and reason without the Holy Spirit] is death [death that comprises all the*

miseries arising from sin, both here and hereafter]. But the mind of the [Holy] Spirit is life and [soul] peace [both now and forever]. [That is] because the mind of the flesh [with its carnal thoughts and purposes] is hostile to God, for it does not submit itself to God's law; indeed it cannot.

So then those who are living the life of the flesh [catering to the appetites and impulses of their carnal nature] cannot please or satisfy God, or be acceptable to Him.

—Romans 8:5-8 AMPC

The carnal mind is the source and foundation of dead works which is the source and foundation of ambition. Ambition is dead works, it is anything that is not initiated, inspired, or controlled by God, His Word, or Holy Spirit.

Dreams, goals, desires, plans, purposes, businesses or any endeavor that is not initiated or has its source or motivation from God is a dead work and it is ambition. Ambitions may look good but there are fatal consequences to them.

You have to decide whether you are going to live by vision or ambition. The choice is yours. I will encourage you to pursue and aggressively follow the path of vision.

It is time for you to set your affection on God and be Spirit driven and controlled so you can became a mighty instrument in the hands of God to carry out and fulfill the will of God in your generation.

CHAPTER THREE

THE FATAL CONSEQUENCES OF AMBITION

The story of two fathers in the scriptures and their choices gives us a clear revelation of the fatal consequences of ambition and also the blessings of a God-given vision. Let us quickly look at these fathers and the choices they made.

Abraham had been through a lot in life. He had the call of God and a seven-fold blessing of God upon his life. He was a covenant friend and partner of God but he went through seasons of famine. The famines and the events of life and the choices he made strategically positioned him for a supernatural transfer of wealth, but he had his nephew Lot with him.

And Abram went up out of Egypt, he, and his wife, and all that he had, and Lot with him, into the south. And Abram was very rich in cattle, in silver, and in gold. And he went on his journeys from the south even to Bethel, unto the place where his tent had been at the beginning, between Bethel and Hai.

Unto the place of the altar, which he had make there at the first: and there Abram called on the name of the Lord. And Lot also, which went with Abram, had flocks, and herds, and tents. And the land was not able to bear them, that they might dwell together: for their substance was great, so that they could not dwell together.

And there was a strife between the herdmen of Abram's cattle and Lot's cattle: and the Canaanite and the Perrizite dwelled then in the land. And Abram said unto Lot, Let there be no strife, I pray thee, between me and thee, and between my herdmen and thy herdmen, for we be brethren.

Is not the whole land before thee? separate thyself, I pray thee, from me: if thou wilt take the left hand, then I will go to the right; or if thou depart to the right hand, then I will go to the left.

—Genesis 13:1-9

Abraham began to experience a strong and undeniable manifestation of the generational blessing he carried. The blessing of the Lord upon him also rubbed off on his nephew Lot who also got blessed because of his association with Abraham. This is a manifestation of the law of association and influence. If you walk with the wise you will be wise. If you walk with the blessed, you will be blessed.

He that walketh with the wise men shall be wise: but a companion of fools shall be destroyed.

—Proverbs 13:20

In the midst of the manifestation of material and financial blessings, the two men could not live together because the land could not handle the magnitude of their wealth. You have to understand that sure blessings always have tangible manifestations.

There was a quarrel between the herdmen of Abraham and the herdmen of Lot. It could have been over wells or grazing pastures or trade. The scriptures do not go into details about that.

Abraham being a peacemaker and a spiritual man encouraged his nephew Lot to separate himself from him to avoid bitterness and contentions. He said to Lot, "The whole land is before you. Choose where you want to position yourself."

Now here is where vision or ambition plays out. It plays out in the midst of the choices of life. Whenever you have to make a choice, you will either make choices based on vision or ambition. You will make choices under the influence of divine guidance and direction of the Holy Spirit or you will make choices under the influence of ambition and human will.

You can make choices based on natural experiences, skill, pride, ego, tricks, games, greed, and a hustler's mind set and mentality, or you can make choices based on prophetic directions and the voice of God.

The choice is yours!

Releasing Vision

Whatever choices you make, good or bad, there will be consequences. The story of Abraham and Lot brings to center stage the fatal consequences of carnal choices in the decisions of life.

Now let us look at how Lot made his choices and the progression of his choices and what over a period of time were the fatal consequences of his choices based on ambition and the desire for wealth and prosperity and not the voice of God or the unfolding of vision.

> *And Lot lifted up his eyes, and beheld all the plain of Jordan, that it was well watered every where, before the Lord destroyed Sodom and Gomorrah, even as the garden of the Lord, like the land of Egypt, as thou comest unto Zoar.*
>
> *Then Lot chose him all the plain of Jordan; and Lot journeyed east: and they separated themselves the one from the other. Abram dwelled in the land of Canaan, and Lot dwelled in the cities of the plain, and pitched his tent toward Sodom. But the men of Sodom were wicked and sinners before the Lord exceedingly.*
>
> —Genesis 13:10-13

When the scripture says that "Lot lifted up his eyes," it means that:

- He tried to access the realm of vision.
- He tried to break out of the natural into the supernatural.
- He tried to gain penetration through the sight gate.

- He tried to access the realms of spiritual ascendancy.
- He tried to hear from God.
- He tried to obtain direction and guidance for the future.
- He tried to break through the spiritual resistances and barriers that were contending with his decision-making abilities.
- He tried to break through the forces that were influencing his motives and his choices.

The psalmist said:

> *I will lift up mine eyes unto the hills, from whence cometh my help. My help cometh from the Lord, which made the heaven and earth.*
>
> —Psalm 121:1-2

In times of desperation and critical moments when your back is against the wall, what do you do? What forces influence your choices and decisions? There are supernatural and natural forces that influence decisions and eventually affect the outcome of destinies. You need to know how these forces operate because you will encounter them at different times in your life. Indeed throughout your life, you will have to deal with these very powerful forces that affect generations yet unborn.

Lot's back was against the wall and he desperately needed to make serious decisions that would affect him, his family, his future, his wealth, prosperity, investments, and destiny. This is when people say "I need a word from God." In situations like these, when you say you need a word from God, do you really mean it or are your words only religious cliché or jargon?

When Lot lifted up his eyes the scriptures did not say he encountered God or that he heard from God or received prophetic direction. The scripture says, "And Lot lifted up his eyes, he beheld all the plain of Jordan, that it was well watered every where."

You have to understand that Lot is about to make decisions and choices that will not just affect him but his family, his financial status, his future and his destiny. At this very critical time in his life, even though Lot had lived with Abraham for years and Abraham was a worshiper, an altar builder, and a covenant friend of God, Lot did not learn from Abraham's God-serving lifestyle. Lot was a carnal man with hidden carnal desires. He was looking for the liberty to carry out his carnal and fleshly activities the moment he was free from Abraham's supervision and observation.

Today there are many carnal and fleshly children of God who are just looking for the opportunity to stay away from church. They want the opportunity to stay away from the observation and guidance of a true man or woman of God so they can do the evil they have always wanted to do. Being in church and being under the authority of a true man or woman of God is a bother to them because they don't have the liberty to sin and live the carnal life they have always wanted to live.

They hide and do their stuff and they have a nasty, rebellious attitude toward God and His work. They treat God and His kingdom like beggars who desperately need them, their gifts, talents, money, and influence. This is how the scriptures describe such ones.

And turning the cities of Sodom and Gomorrah into ashes condemned them with an overthrow, making them an ensample unto those that after should live ungodly; And delivered just Lot vexed with the filthy conversation of the wicked:

(For the righteous man dwelling among them, in seeing and hearing, vexed his righteous soul from day to day with their unlawful deeds;) The Lord knoweth how to deliver the godly out of temptations, and to reserve the unjust unto the day of judgment to be punished:

But chiefly them that walk after the flesh in the lust of uncleanness, and despise government. Presumptuous are they, self-willed, they are not afraid to speak evil of dignities. Whereas angels, which are greater in power and might, bring not railing accusation against them before the Lord.

But these, as natural brute beasts, made to be taken and destroyed, speak evil of the things that they understand not; and shall utterly perish in their own corruption; And shall receive the reward of unrighteousness, as they that count it pleasure to riot in the day time. Spots they are and blemishes, sporting themselves with their own deceivings while they feast with you;

Having eyes full of adultery, and that cannot cease from sin; beguiling unstable souls: an heart they have exercised with covetous practices; cursed children: Which have forsaken the right way, and are gone astray, following the way of Balaam the son of Bosor, who loved the wages of unrighteousness:

But was rebuked for his iniquity: the dumb ass speaking with man's voice forbad the madness of the prophet.

—2 Peter 2:6-16

Beloved, Lot was described as a righteous man. He was a nephew to Abraham the friend of God but look at his choices after he "lifted up his eyes."

- He was influenced by what he saw naturally. His choices and his motives were not based on the voice of God or prophetic directions.

- He was very carnal and materialistic; his choices were based on what he could get materially and financially. "Then Lot chose him all the plains of Jordan."

- He saw the plains of Jordan that it was well watered. He knew that his cattle would do well there. Business would boom and he would acquire more wealth and prosperity.

- The next thing you see is that "Lot dwelled in the cities of the plain, and pitched his tent toward Sodom." At this time, Lot is not in Sodom, but he has pitched his tent toward Sodom. Meanwhile, the scriptural description of the men of Sodom is truly appalling and disgusting!

But the men of Sodom were wicked and sinners before the Lord exceedingly.

—Genesis 13:13

- Finally, Lot is sitting at the gate of Sodom when the Lord sent his angels to carry out a divine investigation inside a cursed city that was on the verge of divine judgment. Lot is now a governor, mayor, senator, politician, or elder in the city of Sodom. You do not sit at the gates of the city if you are not a legislator, lawmaker, or ruler in the city.

Lot had influence and political power in a city whose men were wicked before the Lord exceedingly! These are the fatal progression of events that lead to the fatal consequences of the choices and decisions made out of ambition and not vision.

Remember, the scriptures describe Lot as a righteous man whose soul was vexed from day to day, hearing and seeing the wicked deeds of those evil men.

But the million dollar question is "How did the righteous man end up in such fatality?"

- He was caught in a cross fire of the battle of the nations (Gen. 14:1-12).

- He was taken captive in the midst of the cross fire of the battle of the nations.

And they took all the goods of Sodom and Gomorrah, and all their victuals, and went their way. And they took Lot, Abram's brother's son, who dwelt in Sodom, and his goods, and departed.

—Genesis 14:11-12

- He ended up living in a city that was on God's prophetic agenda for judgment.

And the Lord said, Because the cry of Sodom and Gomorrah is great, and because their sin is very grievous; I will go down now and see whether they have done altogether according to the cry of it, which is come unto me; and if not, I will know.
—Genesis 18:20-21

- Lot is finally a leader, elder, governor, or politician in a city on the verge of divine judgment. He is sitting at the gate of the city when the angels of God came to carry out a divine investigation concerning the cry of the city that had come up before God.

And there came two angels to Sodom at even, and Lot sat in the gate of Sodom: and Lot seeing them rose up to meet them; and bowed himself with his face toward the ground; And he said, Behold now, my lords, turn in, I pray you, into your servants house, and tarry all night, and wash your feet, and ye shall rise up early, and go your ways. And they said, Nay; but we will abide in the street all night. And he pressed upon them greatly; and they turned in unto him, and entered into his house; and he made them a feast, and did bake unleavened bread, and they did eat.

But before they lay down, the men of the city, even the men of Sodom, compassed the house round, both old and young, all the people from every quarter: And they called unto Lot, and said unto him, Where are the men which came in to thee this night? bring them out unto us, that we may know them.

And Lot went out at the door unto them, and shut the door after him, And said, I pray you, brethren, do not so wickedly. Behold now, I have two daughters which have not known man; let me, I pray you, bring them out unto you, and do ye to them as is good in your eyes: only unto these men do nothing; for therefore come they under the shadow of my roof.

And they said, Stand back. And they said again, This one fellow came in to sojourn, and he will needs be a judge: now will we deal worse with thee, than with them. And they pressed sore upon the man, even Lot, and came near to break the door.

But the men put forth their hand, and pulled Lot into the house to them, and shut the door. And they smote the men that were at the door with blindness, both small and great: so that they wearied themselves to find the door.

And the men said unto Lot, Hast thou here any besides? son in law, and thy sons, and thy daughters and whatsoever thou hast in the city, bring them out of this place: For we will destroy this place, because the cry of them is waxen great before the Lord; and the Lord has sent us to destroy it.

Then the Lord rained upon Sodom and Gomorrah brimstone and fire from the Lord out of heaven; And he overthrew those cities and all the plain, and all the inhabitants of the cities, and that which grew upon the ground.

> *But his (Lot's) wife looked back from behind him, and she became a pillar of salt.*
>
> —Genesis 19:1-13, 24-26

These are the fatal consequences of ambition. Lot lost everything, including his wife who became a pillar of salt! It didn't begin at judgment. It began when he had a very important decision to make. Lot lifted up his eyes and beheld the plains of Jordan and they were well watered. They looked green and prosperous, so he followed his ambition and not vision.

Beloved, not everything that glitters is gold!

Lot failed in the art of inquiring of God. He was a righteous man but he was carnal. He had a carnal and unrenewed mind and when he had the opportunity, his carnality kicked in to full force.

You have seen the fatal consequences of ambition and carnality. I pray for you today, that Almighty God will show you mercy and deliver you and every dimension of your life and destiny from carnality, from fleshly activities, pride, egotism, foolishness, dangerous moves and endeavors, and ambition.

It is time to aggressively seek God and come into the realm of vision.

CHAPTER FOUR

GENERATIONAL BLESSINGS

The Product of Vision

The story of two fathers in the scriptures and their choices give us a clear revelation of the fatal consequences of ambition. They also give us an understanding and revelation on the blessings of vision.

You have just seen the fatal consequences of ambition. Now you are about to encounter the source of generational blessings, which is from the power of vision.

> *And the Lord said unto Abram, after that Lot was separated from him, Lift up now thine eyes, and look from the place where thou art northward, and southward, and eastward, and westward:*
>
> *For all the land which thou seest, to thee will I give it, and to thy seed for ever. And I will make thy seed as the dust of the*

earth: so that if a man can number the dust of the earth, then shall thy seed also be numbered.

Arise, walk through the land in the length of it and in the breadth of it; for I will give it unto thee. Then Abram removed his tent, and came and dwelt in the plain of Mamre, which is in Hebron, and built there an altar unto the Lord.

—Genesis 13:14-18

The golden nuggets of spiritual truth to be gleaned out of this portion of scripture is amazing. These are timeless truths that endure from generation to generation.

The first thing you see is a beautiful and loving relationship between Almighty God and His covenant partner and friend Abraham. Remember, God doesn't just step out of his hiding place, out of the realm of the supernatural, the realm of eternity and visit just anybody at all.

He must be in love with you to visit you. You must have done something to attract the presence of God. Today, people just expect to be able to access the realm of vision. They expect God just to step out of eternity and visit them and give them whatever they want.

People don't care about God or the will of God. They just want to use God. This is a generation of users and abusers, and they are not even scared to use, abuse, and misuse God, His presence, His power, His gifts, His wealth, and anything else that belongs to God.

I have some advice for you. God knows your heart. You can deceive everybody but not the Most High God, so do not try to deceive Him. He knows your heart and your motives.

And thou shalt remember all the way which the Lord thy God led thee these forty years in the wilderness, to humble thee, and to prove thee, to know what is in thine heart, whether thou wouldest keep his commandments, or no.

—Deuteronomy 8:2

The heart is deceitful above all things, and desperately wicked: who can know it? I the Lord search the heart, I try the reins, even to give every man according to his ways, and according to the fruit of his doings.

—Jeremiah 17:9-10

Every way of a man is right in his own eyes: but the Lord pondereth the hearts.

—Proverbs 21:2

The reason Abraham could attract the presence of God was because he was a true worshiper. The scripture reveals that Abraham was an altar builder.

- An altar is a meeting place between the natural and the supernatural.
- An altar is a meeting place between humanity and divinity.
- An altar is a meeting place between flesh and spirits (in this case Almighty God who is a Spirit).

- An altar is a meeting place where sacrifices are offered to invoke the presence of a supreme being (in this case Almighty God — Jehovah).

- An altar is a meeting place where covenants are ratified.

- An altar is a meeting place between the covenanter (Almighty God) and the covenantee (in this case Abraham).

- An altar is a meeting place where covenant promises and blessings are activated, released, and imparted.

The issue of altars is serious! You cannot build an altar if you do not have a revelation of the supernatural being you want to meet or encounter at the altar. The strength and power of the altar is based on the strength, power, invincibility, supremacy, and dominion of the supernatural being you want to meet and encounter at the altar.

Today, people have no fear of God, so they treat him any way they wish. They want God to crawl after them and beg them to worship Him. It will never happen. God is too mighty and powerful to come down to your level to beg you to worship him.

There are blessings in being a true and genuine worshiper.

- Worship is to prostrate oneself in humble submission and deep reverence in your heart to Almighty God.

- Worship is to stand and gaze in awe at the glorious magnificence and majestic countenance of the Most High

God, the creator of the universe and to declare to Him how great He is!

- Worship is to serve God with all the gifts and treasures He has endowed you with. This is where ministry comes in. You cannot perform the third if you have not done the first two.

Today there is a serious lack of true worshipers. Abraham was an altar builder, a true worshiper, and because of his genuine heart of worship he was able to attract the presence of God and the power of generational blessings.

Look at God's testimony about Abraham and you will discover why Abraham was able to access the realm of vision and then generational blessings.

And the Lord said, Shall I hide from Abraham that thing which I do; Seeing that Abraham shall surely become a great and mighty nation, and all the nations of the earth shall be blessed by him?

For I know him, that he will command his children and his household after him, and they shall keep the way of the Lord, to do justice and judgment; that the Lord may bring upon Abraham that which he hath spoken of him.

And the Lord said, Because the cry of Sodom and Gomorrah is great, and because their sin is very grievous; I will go down now, and see whether they have done altogether according to the cry of it, which is come unto me, and if not, I will know.

—Genesis 18:17-22

> *And Abraham drew near, and said, Wilt thou also destroy the righteous with the wicked? Peradventure there be fifty righteous within the city: wilt thou also destroy and not spare the place for the fifty righteous that are therein?*
>
> *That be far from thee to do after this manner, to slay the righteous with the wicked: and that the righteous should be as the wicked, that be far from thee: Shall not the Judge of all the earth do right?*
>
> *And the Lord said, If I find in Sodom fifty righteous within the city, then I will spare all the place for their sakes.*
>
> —Genesis 18:23-26

Just look at the beauty of the relationship between Abraham and God. These are two friends talking. Almighty God, I mean Almighty God said, " Shall I hide from Abraham that thing which I do…" (Gen.18:17). God didn't hide his plans of judgment from his friend Abraham.

Jehovah, Almighty God was snitching on Himself. The relationship between Him and Abraham was so intimate that He had to consult with His confidant before carrying out His plans.

In this portion of scripture, you see Abraham walking in the office of a prophet. He had the ability and the capacity to draw near to God. Not only did he draw near to God, he could talk with God as a true confidant and hold God accountable. Sometimes he even would diplomatically rebuke God. He said, "That be far from thee, shall the Judge of all the earth not do right?"

I mean who can talk to God like that? Only men like Abraham and Moses could hold God to those levels of accountability in intercession for nations for God to say things like "Let me alone" (Deut. 32:10).

These were prophets who, because of their track record of humility and faithfulness and their intercession for nations, He would visit and consult with them.

God did not speak with Abraham as long as Lot was around.

And the Lord said unto Abram, after that Lot was separated from him, Lift up now thine eyes, and look from the place where thou art.

—Genesis 13:14a

Lot means a veil. There are some people who are Lots in your life. As long as they are around, they will blur your vision! Their influence casts spells of witchcraft on your spiritual sight. Witchcraft comes from a word in the original language "vasconi," which means to smite with the eye. This is where evil eyes, spells, charms, incantations, enchantments, divinations, sorceries, and necromancies operate.

God will not even bother to speak to you when there is a Lot around you. Is there a Lot around you? Are there some Lots around you? Could that be why you are struggling to hear from God? Could those be the reason your vision has been taken away from you? Separate yourself from Lot and the veil over your sight or your vision will be broken and destroyed!

I prophesy against any Lot in your life. I command the hand of God to uproot them, dislodge them, and relocate them! I command every Lot in your life to be divinely displaced, and I command their evil influence over your life to be broken and destroyed so your vision will be restored!

I command all the adversaries blocking your sight gate to be dislodged, uprooted, destroyed, and cast down. I command all the invisible barriers over your sight and the power of your sight gate to be broken and destroyed by the power of a barrier-breaking anointing.

I command your vision to be restored. I command the voice of God to be clear to you again. I command the restoration of the clarity of vision. You will not see men like trees. I command and release the mystery of the second touch. You will see men like men. You will see clearly.

> *And he took the blind man by the hand, and led him out of the town; and when he had spit on his eyes, and put his hands upon him, he asked him if he saw ought. And he looked up, and said, I see men as trees, walking.*
>
> *After he put his hands again upon his eyes, and made him look up: and he was restored, and saw every man clearly.*
>
> —Mark 8:23-25

There is power in a clear vision. A clear vision boosts moral. A clear vision allows cooperation. A clear vision assists in evaluation. A clear vision empowers and lifts you into new dimensions of divine exploits and destiny!

When Lot was separated from Abraham, God began to release generational blessings! Remember, "The blessing of the Lord, it maketh rich and he addeth no sorrow with it" (Prov. 10:22).

For all the land which thou seest, to thee will I give it, and to thy seed forever. And I will make thy seed as the dust of the earth: so that if a man can number the dust of the earth, then shall thy seed also be numbered. Arise, walk through the land in the length of it and in the breadth of it; for I will give it to thee.

—Genesis 13:16-17

When you are an altar builder and you build your altars, you will attract God to come on the scene with His power activating and ratifying the covenants of blessings.

Remember:

- There can be no abundance or prosperity if there is no blessing.
- There can be no blessing if there is no covenant.
- There can be no covenant if there is no sacrifice.
- There can be no sacrifice if there is no altar.
- There can be no altar if there is no revelation.

Revelation is critical. Revelation is pivotal. Revelation is crucial. Revelation is the foundation for divine encounters and the activation of covenant blessings. Revelation is the master key that gives access to the realm of vision to release generational blessings and the promises of God.

Releasing Vision

Where there is no vision, people perish. They live carelessly and they walk aimlessly. Your days of failure are over. There is no situation, problem, challenge, difficulty, or impossibility that the power of God cannot deal with but the million dollar questions are:

- Are you a friend of God?

- Are you an altar builder?

- Are you a true worshiper?

- Are you one who operates in different dimensions of sacrifice?

- Are you in covenant with Almighty God, the Father of our Lord Jesus Christ?

If your answer is yes to all the above, generational blessings are your portion. If the answer is no to any of the above questions, then you have some work to do. Your work must start with searching your heart and getting rid of all sin, idols and carnality so you can come to a place of total surrender to God and His plans.

CHAPTER FIVE

THE PLANS AND PURPOSES OF GOD

Vision is only obtained in the spiritual or supernatural realm. Remember, God is a Spirit and He operates from the spiritual or supernatural realm.

Therefore, to encounter God you have to cross over the barriers and limitations of the physical or natural realm and make your way into the spiritual or supernatural realm. Then and only then can you hear the voice of God, understand His plans and purposes, and encounter His counsel by revelation.

Many people live and die without ever having an encounter with God to obtain His plans and purposes for their lives. They do whatever they want to do, live wherever they want to live, and work wherever they want to work without ever asking God what His plans and thoughts are for their lives.

Then the word of the Lord came unto me, saying, Before I formed thee in the belly I knew thee; and before thou camest forth out of the womb I sanctified thee, and I ordained thee a prophet unto the nations.

—Jeremiah 1:4-5

In the scripture above, God was revealing His plans and purposes to Jeremiah through a prophetic word, "Then the word of the Lord came unto me, saying." This is so important. The word of the Lord must come to you! You need a word from God. You need to hear from God! Without His counsel, you will live carelessly and aimlessly without purpose and vision.

When the word of the Lord came to Jeremiah, God began to speak to him about events that occurred before he was formed in the belly. God said to Jeremiah, "I knew thee; and before thou camest forth out of the womb I sanctified thee, and I ordained thee a prophet unto the nations."

Jeremiah's call began even before he was formed in the belly. It is important for you to recognize that you are not here by chance. You are not a mistake. Your father and mother could make a mistake, but God never makes mistakes. He sent you here on a mission, and it is important for you to discover the reason for your being.

God said to Jeremiah, "I sanctified thee, and I ordained thee a prophet unto the nations." Here God revealed His counsel to Jeremiah. This was not done in the natural. All of this was occurring in the supernatural and prophetic realm, the realm where divine encounters and visions occur.

> *For I know the thoughts that I think toward you, saith the Lord, thoughts of peace, and not of evil, to give you an expected end.*
> —Jeremiah 29:11

Beloved, God has thoughts toward you too. God has plans and purposes for your life. You are not here because you want to be here. God sent you here with a mission and an assignment. You must discover your purpose and destiny!

God has given you "an expected end." This speaks about your destiny! God has planned your life—from beginning to end—to go a certain way.

> *Remember the former things of old: for I am God, and there is none else; I am God, and there is none like me, Declaring the end from the beginning, and from ancient times the things that are not yet done, saying, My counsel shall stand, and I will do all my pleasure.*
>
> *Calling a ravenous bird from the east, the man that executeth my counsel from a far country: yea I have spoken it, I will also bring it to pass; I have purposed it, I will also do it.*
> —Isaiah 46:9-11

He is the God who declares the end from the beginning. He is the Alpha and the Omega at the same time. He is the Beginning and the End at the same time. He is the omnipresent, omniscient and omnipotent God. None can be compared to Him.

He created time! He is the self-existent God who exists in eternity. He created everything that is in existence today including time, where mankind exists. God exists in eternity; those on earth exist in time. He is bigger than time, He controls time, the universe, the galaxies, and everything else that exists, both seen and unseen. He deserves all worship and adoration!

The unfolding of the mystery of vision occurs when the Most High and Almighty God decides to reveal His plans, purposes, and counsel to you. The plans, purposes, and counsel of God is what He thought and purposed to do with your life before you were born, before you were even formed in your mother's womb.

The Lord of hosts hath sworn, saying, Surely as I have thought, so shall it come to pass; and as I have purposed, so shall it stand. For the Lord of hosts hath purposed, and who shall disannul it? and his hand is stretched out, and who shall turn it back?

—Isaiah 14:24, 27

God has plans for individuals, families, communities, cities, nations, and generations. The plans and purposes of God have to be discovered, and they can only be discovered in the supernatural realm.

God has plans and purposes which He is determined to bring to pass from generation to generation. The discovery of the plans and purposes of God is the unfolding of the mystery of vision.

You have already seen from scripture that vision and God's plans and purposes can only be obtained in the supernatural realm, and this has to be done by faith. Faith takes you into the realm of unseen realities. Faith takes you beyond the natural realm into the supernatural realm.

> *Through faith we understand that the worlds were framed by the word of God, so that things which are seen were not made of things which do appear.*
>
> —Hebrews 11:3

This is an important scripture because it lays the foundation of the principles of faith required to access the realm of vision. It confirms that the things we see were not made of things "which do appear."

This implies that physical things (things seen) were made of (things unseen) spiritual things. Let's look at another scripture that will help you as you journey into the spiritual, the supernatural realm.

> *While we look not at the things which are seen, but at the things which are not seen: for the things which are seen are temporal; but the things which are not seen are eternal.*
>
> —2 Corinthians 4:18

This scripture offers strong encouragement to look at some things and not at others. This scripture says:

- Do not focus your attention on things that are seen.

- Focus your attention on things that are not seen.

Releasing Vision

This is where more million-dollar questions arise! *Are there things which cannot be seen?* and *How do I focus my attention on things which are not seen?*

The answer is yes. There are things which cannot be seen, these are spiritual things. For example, angels cannot be seen physically, but they do exist. Demons cannot be seen physically, but they do exist. So there are things which exist and operate in the spiritual or supernatural realm. That is the same realm where vision is revealed.

Now if you want to come into the spiritual, or supernatural realm you need to know what to do to get there. On the other hand, if you want God to step out of that realm which is the supernatural realm, you need to know what to do to activate the visitations of God and His presence.

CHAPTER SIX

THE CRISIS

Without an encounter with God, you cannot receive a vision. In order to have an encounter with God, you have to focus on things unseen, spiritual and supernatural things.

In the beginning when God made man in His image and after His likeness, He frequently came into the Garden of Eden to visit man. One day He came in and kept calling Adam and there was no response. When Adam responded, he said he was hiding. This is where the crisis of hearing the voice of God and gaining access into the realm of vision began.

> *And the serpent said unto the woman, Ye shall not surely die: For God doth know that in the day ye eat thereof, then your eyes shall be opened, and ye shall be as gods, knowing good and evil.*
>
> *And when the woman saw that the tree was good for food, and that it was pleasant to the eyes, and a tree to be desired to make one wise, she took of the fruit thereof, and did eat, and gave also unto her husband with her, and he did eat.*

And the eyes of them both were opened, and they knew that they were naked; and they sewed fig leaves together, and made themselves aprons. And they heard the voice of the Lord God walking in the garden in the cool of the day: and Adam and his wife hid themselves from the presence of the Lord God amongst the trees of the garden.

And the Lord God called unto Adam, and said unto him, Where art thou? And he said, I heard thy voice in the garden, and I was afraid, because I was naked; and I hid myself.

And he said, Who told thee that thou wast naked? Hast thou eaten of the tree, whereof I commanded thee that thou shouldest not eat? And the man said, The woman whom thou gavest to be with me, she gave me of the tree, and I did eat. And the Lord God said unto the woman, What is this that thou has done? And the woman said, The serpent beguiled me, and I did eat.

And the Lord God said unto the serpent, Because thou hadst done this, thou art cursed above all cattle, and above every beast of the field; upon thy belly shalt thou go, and dust shall thou eat all the days of thy life:

And I will put enmity between thee and the woman, and between thy seed and her seed; it shall bruise thy head, and thou shall bruise his heel.

Therefore the Lord God sent him forth from the garden of Eden, to till the ground from whence he was taken. So he drove out the man; and he placed at the east of the garden of Eden Cherubims, and a flaming sword which turned every way, to keep the way of the tree of life.

—Genesis 3:4-15, 23-24

This is the foundation of the crisis, the crisis of not having access to God's presence, and consequently to the voice and communication of God. This is a major crisis because God drove man from His presence and positioned angels with flaming swords to block man from His presence.

You have to understand that Eden was not just a physical location or just a garden.

- Eden was where the glory and presence of God manifested.
- Eden was a realm of creativity and productivity.
- Eden was a realm of abundance and prosperity.
- Eden was a realm of power, dominion, and authority.
- Eden was a realm of favor and miracles.
- Eden was a realm of peace and joy.
- Eden was a realm of the supernatural blessings of God.

When man was driven out of Eden, he was not just driven out of a physical or geographical location. He was driven out of:

- The realm of the presence of God.
- The realm of creativity and productivity.
- The realm of abundance and prosperity.

- The realm of power, dominion, and authority.
- The realm of favor and miracles.
- The realm of peace and joy.
- The realm of the supernatural blessings of God.

After man became naked, he lost the glory and presence of God. The glory and presence of God was his mantle! The mantle gave him the ability to communicate with God. He could hear the voice of God and understand His plans and purposes.

With the mantle, man had clarity of vision and every supernatural equipment he needed to function and succeed in his mission as God's delegated authority and representative upon the earth.

When he lost the glory, the mantle, and the presence of God, he was reduced to a lower rank of dignity, authority, and dominion.

- He went from spiritual life to spiritual death.
- He went from blessings into curses.
- He went from riches into poverty.
- He went from victory to defeat.
- He went from success to failure.
- He went from health to sickness.
- He went from the supernatural to the natural.

This was a major crisis, one that has passed on from generation to generation. It is the source of trouble, pain, anguish, sorrow, rejection, rebellion, poverty, suicide, murder, anger, wars, contentions, hatred, bitterness, envy, jealousy, and the endless list of all evil.

Under these conditions man, instead of being a spiritual man who could navigate with skill and dominion in the supernatural realm and have fellowship and communion with God, was now barred and blocked from the realm of the supernatural. He ended up as a natural man who could not hear the voice of God or receive visitations from God.

This was the most devastating occurrence to the plans and purposes of God. But God in His infinite wisdom had already put in place the plan and blessing of redemption.

> *Christ hath redeemed us from the curse of the law, being made a curse for us: for it is written, Cursed is every one that hangeth on a tree: That the blessing of Abraham might come on the Gentiles through Jesus Christ; that we might receive the promise of the Spirit through faith.*
> —Galatians 3:13-14

When you give your life to Christ, there is restoration of all that the first Adam lost. Legally, you are adopted back into the family of God and you become a child of God, and through the blessings of redemption you receive restoration of the mantle and the presence of God.

Releasing Vision

> *For since by man came death, by man came also the resurrection of the dead. For as in Adam all die; even so in Christ shall all be made alive.*
>
> —1 Corinthians 15:21-22

When you give your life to Christ, the Holy Spirit, the Spirit of Glory, comes to reside in you and the glory of God that is the manifested presence of God that the first Adam had is now your portion! There is the restoration of glory!

> *But if the Spirit of him that raised up Jesus from the dead dwell in you, he that raised up Christ from the dead shall also quicken your mortal bodies by his Spirit that dwelleth in you.*
>
> —Romans 8:11

> *Know ye not that ye are the temple of God, and that the Spirit of God dwelleth in you?*
>
> —1 Corinthians 3:16

> *If ye be reproached for the name of Christ, happy are ye; for the spirit of glory and of God resteth upon you: on their part he is evil spoken of but on your part he is glorified.*
>
> —1 Peter 4:14

It is time for you to take advantage of the different dimensions of the Spirit of God's operations. He dwells and lives within you, He comes upon you to empower you for service. He is with you and for you all the days of your life.

> *What shall we then say to these things? If God be for us, who can be against us? He that spared not his own Son, but*

delivered him up for us all, how shall he not with him also freely give us all things?

Who shall lay anything to the charge of God's elect? It is God that justifieth. Who is he that condemneth? It is Christ that died, yea rather, that is risen again, who is even at the right hand of God, who also maketh intercession for us.

Who shall separate us from the love of Christ? shall tribulation, or distress, or persecution, or famine, or nakedness, or peril, or sword? As it is written, For thy sake we are killed all the day long; we are accounted as sheep for the slaughter.

Nay, in all these things we are more than conquerors through him that loved us.

—Romans 8:31-37

CHAPTER SEVEN

SUPERNATURAL TRANSPORTATION

The manifested presence of God was the mantle, vesture, or apparel that Adam wore. As long as he had it on, he could access the realm of God, which is the supernatural realm. He could hear the voice of God and operate in the realm of vision.

> *What is man, that thou art mindful of him? and the son of man, that thou visitest him? For thou hast made him a little lower than the angels, and hast crowned him with glory and honor. Thou madest him to have dominion over the works of thy hands; thou hast put all things under his feet.*
>
> —Psalm 8:4-6

Man was God's delegated authority upon the earth, and he had to stay in constant fellowship and communication with God. He had to know the plans and purposes of God so he could execute the counsel of God upon the earth.

Releasing Vision

The mantle he wore, which was the glory and the presence of God, enabled him to access and operate in that realm. In the scriptures you discover people who were able to access the realm of vision and encounter the plans and purposes of God.

Today, you can access that realm of vision through the agency and ministry of the Holy Spirit. If you seek God, He will reveal His plans and purposes to you like He did for Joseph.

Joseph was a young man who, after his father had made a coat of many colors for him, began to have dreams and visions. Through dreams and visions, God revealed His plans and purposes to Joseph concerning things God had already revealed to Abraham in a vision. When the time for the fulfillment of His counsel came into manifestation, God visited Pharaoh through dreams and visions, and only Joseph could interpret them!

None of the magicians, astrologers, diviners, necromancers, sorcerers, or wise men in Egypt could interpret the king's dreams. Joseph's interpretation brought about his promotion and exaltation, he became second in command in Egypt, a land in which he was a stranger. When this occurred, Joseph's own dreams came to pass.

> **I prophesy and declare that this is your season of a supernatural raise and a divine lift that will strategically position you for the manifestation of your prophetic destiny.**

Now Israel loved Joseph more than all his children, because he was the son of his old age: and he made for him a coat of many colors. And when his brethren saw that their father loved him more than all his brethren, they hated him, and could not speak peaceably unto him.

And Joseph dreamed a dream, and he told it his brethren: and they hated him yet the more. And he said unto them, Here, I pray you, this dream which I have dreamed: For, behold, we were binding sheaves in the field, and, lo, my sheaf arose, and also stood upright; and, behold your sheaves stood round about, and made obeisance to my sheaf.

—Genesis 37:3-7

The coat of many colors that Jacob made for his son Joseph is a type of:

- Ministry of the Holy Spirit.

- Priestly anointing.

- Kingship anointing.

- Prophetic anointing.

- Mantle and its operations.

There is no record of Joseph dreaming or accessing the realm of vision until he wore the coat of many colors. This is a very important truth to embrace seriously and adhere to. Without the Holy Spirit, His enablement and empowerment, you are stuck on ground zero. You will never take off!

When Joseph wore the coat of many colors, he gained access into the realm of vision. He began to dream, and his dreams provoked his brothers to anger, hatred, envy, and jealousy.

The coat of many colors, which was a type of different kinds of anointing, brought into manifestation the operation of spiritual gifts. In the life of Joseph, through his dreams and visions, you discover the operation of some of the gifts of revelation and the gift of prophecy. These supernatural gifts only began to operate *after* he wore the coat of many colors.

The mantle empowered Joseph and lifted him into the realms of supernatural transportation. Spiritual gifts are very powerful; they determine the outcome of one's destiny.

A man's gift maketh room for him, and bringeth him before great men.

—Proverbs 18:16

Spiritual gifts are no respecter of persons. Once the atmosphere is right, the gift will operate. Supernatural gifts or spiritual gifts are a manifestation of the grace of God and wherever grace manifests the sovereignty of God is in operation.

God gives grace and supernatural gifts to whoever He wants to, according to His purpose and destiny, and He doesn't have to seek counsel or consult with anyone about what He decides to do with whoever. Joseph's brothers were angry and hated him for the coat of many colors and the supernatural gifts that began to operate in his life.

Now Israel loved Joseph more than all his children, because he was the son of his old age: and he made for him a coat of many colours. And when his brethren saw that their father loved him more than all his brethren, they hated him, and could not speak peaceably unto him.

And Joseph dreamed a dream, and he told it his brethren: and they hated him yet the more. And he said unto them, Hear, I pray you, this dream which I have dreamed: For, behold, we were binding sheaves in the field, and lo, my sheaf arose, and also stood upright; and, behold, your sheaves stood round about, and made obeisance to my sheaf.

And his brethren said to him, Shalt thou indeed reign over us? or shalt thou indeed have dominion over us? And they hated him yet the more for his dreams, and for his words.

And he dreamed yet another dream, and told it his brethren, and said, Behold, I have dreamed a dream more; and, behold, the sun and the moon and the eleven stars made obeisance to me.

And he told it to his father, and to his brethren: and his father rebuked him, and said unto him, What is this dream that thou hast dreamed? Shall I and thy mother and thy brethren indeed come to bow down ourselves to thee to the earth?

And his brethren envied him; but his father observed the saying.

—Genesis 37:3-11

Supernatural gifts were in operation in Joseph's life. He was dreaming and the dreams were a revelation of the counsel of God. God had entered into covenant with Abraham and told him that his seed would be strangers in a land that was not theirs, and they would be afflicted for four hundred years, but they would come out, and they would not come out empty.

It is important for you to know that the emotions or moods of Joseph's brethren could not stop his gifts from operating. Joseph's brothers hated him because he was his father's favorite, and his father, Jacob, did not hide his special love for Joseph.

Parents, you have to be careful about how you treat your children because favoritism can cause a lot of problems in a family. It can release spirits of rejection, bitterness, resentment, anger, envy, jealousy, and many more.

If the family situations are very bad, it can end up in suicide or murder. Parents please be careful. Joseph was the son of his father's old age, not because he was the youngest child, but because he really served his father well and paid attention to his father's needs in his old age. Benjamin was younger than Joseph, but he was not called the son of Jacob's old age.

Joseph brought all the evil report of his brothers to his father. He was, in today's terms, a business manager, an accountant or an auditor who was able to discern all the unscrupulous practices of his brethren in regards to trade, business, and the family estates. In view of his diligence and loyalty the old man, Jacob could not hide his special love and appreciation for his favorite son. He made a coat of many colors for him. It was designer made, and it was very unique and expensive. It symbolized that he was heir of the family inheritance. Joseph, even though he was the eleventh son, qualified for the birthright, which by custom and tradition belonged to the firstborn.

He possessed the birthright and the double portion of the natural and supernatural inheritance of the covenant blessings because of his character and qualities of faithfulness, loyalty, and diligence amongst many others. Even though Reuben was the firstborn, and the double portion always went to the firstborn, he was disqualified and Joseph received the double portion.

> *Reuben, thou art my firstborn, my might, and the beginning of my strength, the excellency of dignity, and the excellency of power: Unstable as water, thou shalt not excel; because thou wentest up to thy father's bed; then defiledst thou it: he went up to my couch.*
> —Genesis 49:3-4

> *Now the sons of Reuben the firstborn of Israel, (for he was the firstborn; but forasmuch as he defiled his father's bed, his birthright was given unto the sons of Joseph the son of Israel: and the genealogy is not to be reckoned after the birthright. For Judah prevailed above his brethren, and of him came the chief ruler; but the birthright was Joseph's:)*
> —1 Chronicles 5:1-2

The dreams of Joseph were the operations of the gift of the word of knowledge, the gift of the word of wisdom, and the gift of prophecy. The gift of the word of knowledge reveals events of the present and the past and the gift of the word of wisdom reveals events of the future. Prophecy is a revelation of the mind of God on different levels.

Prophecies are supernatural operations that cannot be obtained though natural knowledge or wisdom. They do not function because of your number of years of learning, education, or degrees you have acquired. These gifts function on a supernatural plane and platform through the ministry of the Holy Spirit.

Joseph was supernaturally transported into the future, into the glorified stage of his life. He was given a glimpse of things that were going to come to pass. These were futuristic events that were going to occur that he had no idea about. He was going to become a ruler in Egypt after he interpreted the dreams of Pharaoh, and while he was a ruler, his brothers were going to come into Egypt because of the famine in the land at that time.

> *Then they speedily took down every man his sack to the ground, and opened every man his sack. And he searched, and began at the eldest, and left at the youngest: and the cup was found in Benjamin's sack.*
>
> *Then they rent their clothes, and laded every man his ass, and returned to the city. And Judah and his brethren came to Joseph's house; for he was yet there: and they fell before him on the ground. And Joseph said unto them, What deed is this that ye have done? wot ye not that such a man as I can certainly divine?*
>
> *And Judah said, What shall we say unto my lord? what shall we speak? or how shall we speak? or how shall we clear*

ourselves? God hath found out the iniquity of thy servants: behold, we are my lord's servants, both we, and he also with whom the cup is found.

And he said, God forbid that I should do so: but the man in whose hand the cup is found, he shall be my servant, and as for you, get you up in peace unto your father.

Then Judah came near unto him, and said, Oh my lord, let thy servant, I pray thee, speak a word in my lord's ears, and let not thine anger burn against thy servant: for thou art even as Pharaoh.

—Genesis 44:11-18

Judah had to go into long explanations about how they couldn't leave Benjamin in Egypt as a captive because he had promised their father Jacob that they were going to bring him back. In the midst of all the events, Joseph's dreams were manifesting right before all of them. It is important for you to realize that when God has plans and purposes, they will come to pass despite the conspiracies and evil agendas of man.

Then Joseph could not refrain himself before all them that stood by him; and he cried, Cause every man to go out from me. And there stood no man with him, while Joseph made himself known to his brethren.

And he wept aloud: and the Egyptians and the house of Pharaoh heard. And Joseph said unto his brethren, I am Joseph; doth my father yet live? And his brethren could not answer him; for they were troubled at his presence.

Releasing Vision

> *And Joseph said unto his brethren, Come near unto me, I pray you. And they came near. And he said, I am Joseph your brother, whom ye sold into Egypt. Now therefore be not grieved, nor angry with yourselves, that ye sold me hither: for God did send me before you to preserve life.*
>
> —Genesis 45:1-5

The brothers of Joseph were flabbergasted. They were troubled and awestricken. They couldn't believe that this was the brother they had sold into slavery. He was now second in command to Pharaoh. God had established His eternal counsel. Joseph's dreams had come to pass. They bowed before Joseph!

Joseph through dreams and visions was supernaturally transported into the past to access the vision Abraham had when God told him that his seed would be strangers in a land that was not theirs and they would be afflicted for four hundred years. This vision of Abraham's and the covenant that God entered into with him was coming to pass.

Joseph, through dreams and visions, was supernaturally transported into the future to see his brothers bowing down to him and his father and the entire family paying obeisance, honor, to him. It is important for you to learn from these great treasures of spiritual truth.

God in His sovereignty is entitled to do whatever He wants to do with whomever He chooses. No man can control the plans, purposes or counsel of God. God will have it the way He wants it, the way He has planned it. Anything evil that any person will attempt to do will only hasten the manifestation of the counsel of God.

The Holy Spirit is the one who can lift you up and supernaturally transport you into the realm of vision. He can do that Himself alone or in collaboration with the hand of the Lord.

> *The hand of the Lord was upon me, and carried me out in the spirit of the Lord, and set me down in the midst of the valley which was full of bones, And caused me to pass by them round about: and, behold, there were very many in the open valley; and, lo, they were very dry.*
>
> *And he said unto me, Son of man, can these bones live? And I answered, O Lord God, thou knowest. Again he said unto me, Prophesy upon these bones, and say unto them, O ye dry bones, hear the word of the Lord.*
>
> *Thus saith the Lord God unto these bones; Behold, I will cause breath to enter into you, and ye shall live:*
> —Ezekiel 37:1-5

Ezekiel the prophet, just like Joseph, came under the influence of the Spirit and the hand of the Lord and was supernaturally transported or propelled into the realm of vision. When he got into that realm of vision, he saw things the ordinary person did not see.

Ezekiel was enabled and empowered to access the prophetic realm, the realm of vision, and he was directed as to how to operate in that realm.

It is important for you to know that there are many operations and activities of the Holy Spirit, but this activity of supernatural transportation is very unique and special.

- You cannot force yourself to access the realm of vision.
- You cannot force yourself to dream.
- You cannot conjure or manufacture dreams and visions.
- You cannot walk in assumption or presumption in regard to dreams and visions.
- You cannot force yourself to see into the supernatural or spiritual realm.

The Holy Spirit has to supernaturally transport, propel, or lift you into that realm. This is why an intimate relationship with the Holy Spirit is very important. The Holy Spirit has to be your friend, and you must have deep reverence and respect for Him, His wishes, and desires.

Today so many people want to walk and operate in the prophetic realm of dreams and visions without respect and reverence for the Holy Spirit and the plans and purposes of God. Grieving and quenching the Holy Spirit can be very costly. You can lose the mantle or reduce the authenticity and authority of the mantle.

When you are supernaturally transported into the realm of vision, the plans and purposes of God are revealed to you and you are given prophetic directions as to how to enforce and fulfill those divine assignments.

Joseph was supernaturally transported into the realm of vision and the counsel of God was revealed to him. God entered into a covenant of fire with His friend Abraham, and in the midst of the covenant's ratification, He revealed His plans and purposes to Abraham.

> *And when the sun was going down, a deep sleep fell upon Abram; and, lo, an horror of great darkness fell upon him. And he said unto Abram, Know of a surety that thy seed shall be a stranger in a land that is not theirs, and shall serve them; and they shall afflict them four hundred years; And also that nation, whom they shall serve, will I judge: and afterward shall they come out with great substance.*
>
> *And it came to pass, that, when the sun went down, and it was dark, behold a smoking furnace, and a burning lamp that passed between those pieces. In the same day the Lord made a covenant with Abram, saying, Unto thy seed have I given this land, from the river of Egypt unto the great river, the river Euphrates:*
>
> —Genesis 15:12-14, 17-18

Abraham, during the ratification of a covenant, was supernaturally transported into the realm of vision and prophetically informed about the events of future generations. In the days of Joseph, his life and ministry was the fulfillment of the vision Abraham had seen generations earlier.

Almighty God took Joseph, through the activities of the mantle, into the realm of vision for him to begin to encounter what had been revealed to his great grandfather Abraham, which were the plans and purposes of God yet to manifest.

The unfolding, or the revelation, of vision is the manifestation of the plans and purposes of God. You must be supernaturally transported into that realm of vision by the Holy Spirit.

He is a generational God who carries out His counsel from generation to generation. The unfolding of the mystery of vision is trans-generational. It is from one generation to another.

God has plans and purposes, and He is determined to carry them out. You have to humbly seek God and allow Him to reveal His plans and purposes to you for you to fulfill your assignment and mission in the midst of His great counsel.

Philip the Evangelist

There are different dimensions of supernatural transportation through the activities of the mantle and the operations of the Holy Spirit. In the New Testament there is a record of Philip the evangelist and his ministry to Samaria. During a mighty citywide revival, the angel of the Lord appears to Philip and demands for him to leave a powerful revival of thousands of people and head for the desert. It is important for you to realize that prophetic directions don't always make sense, but if God is giving directions, then there is a divine purpose and it has to be obeyed.

And the angel of the Lord spake unto Philip, saying, Arise, and go toward the south unto the way that goeth down from Jerusalem unto Gaza, which is desert. And he arose and went:

and, behold, a man of Ethiopia, an eunuch of great authority under Candace queen of the Ethiopians, who had the charge of all her treasure, and had come to Jerusalem for to worship. Was returning and sitting in his chariot read Esaias the prophet.

Then the Spirit said unto Philip, Go near, and join thyself to this chariot. And Philip ran thither to him, and heard him read the prophet Esaias, and said, Understandest thou what thou readest? And he said, How can I, except some man should guide me? And he desired Philip that he would come up and sit with him.

Then Philip opened his mouth and began at the same scripture, and preached unto him Jesus. And as they went on their way, they came unto a certain water: and the eunuch said, See, here is water; what doth hinder me to be baptized?

And Philip said, If thou believest with all thine heart, thou mayest. And he answered and said, I believe that Jesus Christ is the Son of God. And he commanded the chariot to stand still: and they went down both into the water, both Philip and the eunuch; and he baptized him. And when they were come up out of the water, the Spirit of the Lord caught away Philip, that the eunuch saw him no more: and he went on his way rejoicing. But Philip was found at Azotus: and passing through he preached in all the cities, till he came to Caesarea.

—Acts 8:26-31; 35-40

"And when they were come out of the water, the Spirit of the Lord caught away Philip, that the eunuch saw him no more." That is supernatural transportation. The words "caught away" are the same words used to describe the rapture that will catch away the saints when the trumpet sounds on that great and powerful day.

Supernatural transportation, whether it is in the prophetic realm during dreams, visions, or diverse gifts of revelation or it is in physical or geographical locations is for specific divine assignments. When God has plans and purposes, He will do whatever He has to do to bring His counsel to pass.

You have to understand that according to church history, this Ethiopian eunuch, who was a minister of secretary of finance for his nation, under the authority of Candace queen of Ethiopia, was a worshiper. He had come to Jerusalem to worship and was on his way back to Africa. This prophetic and evangelistic encounter brought this great politician to Christ.

According to Church history, because of his influence and authority, this man turned 95 percent of his nation to Christ.

> **I command the miracles of supernatural transportation to manifest that will bring great men and women of influence to Christ.**
>
> **I prophesy the supernatural arrest of politicians and great leaders into the kingdom of God. I command national and international revival because men and women of great influence will come to Christ, and that they will not hide their influence but use it to speedily advance the course**

of the gospel of Jesus Christ. That the kingdoms of this world would become the kingdoms of our God and His Christ.

And the seventh angel sounded; and there were great voices in heaven, saying, The kingdoms of this world are become the kingdoms of our Lord, and of his Christ; and he shall reign forever and ever.

—Revelation 11:15

CHAPTER EIGHT

PROPHESY

The prophetic anointing is able to bring back to life anything that is dying or is already dead. When the prophetic anointing is present, the resurrection power of God begins to go into manifestation, natural laws are suspended, and the supernatural takes over.

> *And Elisha died, and they buried him. And the bands of the Moabites invaded the land at the coming in of the year. And it came to pass, as they were burying a man, that, behold, they spied a band of men; and they cast the man into the sepulchre of Elisha: and when the man was let down, and touched the bones of Elisha, he revived, and stood up on his feet.*
> —2 Kings 13:20-21

This is a clear example of how powerful the prophetic anointing operates. Elisha was a mighty anointed prophet of God who in his lifetime and ministry operated in the workings of miracles. In the ministry of Elisha, he raised the dead. In fact, the power of God was so strong in his life that tremendous miracles occurred wherever he went.

Releasing Vision

Remember, Elisha carried a double portion of Elijah's anointing, and Elijah did not die. He was supernaturally transported into heaven. But before he was transported into heaven, he asked Elisha what he wanted.

And it came to pass, when they were gone over, that Elijah said unto Elisha, Ask what I shall do for thee, before I be taken away from thee. And Elisha said, I pray thee, let a double portion of thy spirit be upon me.

And he said, Thou has asked a hard thing: nevertheless, if thou see me when I am taken from thee, it shall be so unto thee; but if not, it shall not be so. And it came to pass, as they still went on, and talked, that, behold, there appeared a chariot of fire, and horses of fire, and parted them both asunder, and Elijah went up by a whirlwind into heaven.

And Elisha saw it, and he cried, My father, my father, the chariot of Israel, and the horsemen thereof. And he saw him no more: and he took hold of his own clothes, and rent them in two pieces.

He took up also the mantle of Elijah that fell from him, and went back, and stood by the bank of Jordan; And he took the mantle of Elijah that fell from him, and smote the waters, and said, Where is the Lord God of Elijah? and when he also had smitten the waters, they parted hither and thither, and Elisha went over.

And when the sons of the prophets which were to view at Jericho saw him, they said, The spirit of Elijah doth rest on

Elisha. And they came to meet him, and bowed themselves to the ground before him.

—2 Kings 2:9-15

This was the beginning of the miracle ministry of Elisha! He had the skills, the capacity, and the inner tenacity to pick up the mantle of Elijah. Elijah knew he was not going to die. He knew he was going to experience supernatural transportation into heaven. He was aware of the timing of his departure from the earth so he told Elisha, "If you see me when I am taken from thee…." He didn't say if you see me when I die.

These men had power over death. There was a strong apostolic, prophetic, and governmental anointing working in their lives that brought into manifestation tremendous miracles. According to the records, only two men did not experience death and they were Elijah and Enoch!

Elisha saw the chariot and horses of fire supernaturally transport Elijah from earth into heaven. In the midst of his flight into heaven, in mid-air, the mantle of Elijah was released from the chariot and it fell upon the earth.

Elisha picked up the mantle of Elijah and tore his own garments and wore the mantle of Elijah. When he got to the river Jordan, he said "Where is the Lord God of Elijah?" Then he took Elijah's mantle and smote the river Jordan, and it parted. Elisha walked through the river on dry ground and went to the other side of the Jordan.

This is a strong manifestation of prophetic power and miracle ministry! This is the kind of miracle anointing that was imparted to Elisha from Elijah through the laws of association and influence. When the prophetic anointing is in manifestation, miracles begin to occur. The impossible becomes possible. Resurrection power moves into manifestation and the spirit of death is overpowered.

When Elisha picked up the mantle of Elijah, the mantle was symbolic of:

- The apostolic and governmental anointing and office that Elijah carried and walked in.

- The prophetic anointing and office with all the relevant spiritual gifts required to function in that office.

- The supernatural wisdom and favor that accompanied the various offices and assignments that Elijah demonstrated in his lifetime.

- The supernatural provision and the workings of miracles that operated in the life and ministry of Elijah.

- The supernatural ability to be supernaturally transported into different dimensions and realms for the manifestation, demonstration, and execution of apostolic, prophetic, and divine assignments.

The mantle of Elijah was symbolic of miracle ministry of which the workings of miracles played a predominant role in that office.

Today, there are many people who want a transference and an impartation of various mantles with their corresponding anointing in their life but are very ignorant of the laws that govern the activation and impartation of mantles!

This is the Elisha who died, and years after his death, they cast a man into his grave. According to the scriptures, "When the man was let down, and touched the bones of Elisha, he revived, and stood up on his feet" (2 Kgs. 13:21b).

This is a raw demonstration and manifestation of resurrection and miracle power. All natural laws were suspended and the supernatural power of God took over. It is important for you to understand that:

- Elisha is dead and has been buried.

- A dead man is put into the grave of the dead prophet.

- The resurrection and miracle power of God after many years is still flowing in the bones of the dead prophet.

- The dead prophet does not wake up to pray or resurrect the dead man. The prophet is still dead.

- The miracle power of God works through the bones of the dead prophet, who has still not woken up and resurrects the dead, and the dead man is raised from the dead. He is revived and stands up on his feet.

This is where all reasoning, logic, mental assent, and carnality is shattered and destroyed. Today, many people want to be analytical and deductive in their approach to God. I hope you are not one of them. If you are, I pray to God that your deliverance is now.

I command you to be delivered from reasoning, rationalizing, sense knowledge, doubt, and unbelief of God and His truths. There are things the natural mind can never fathom or comprehend. The supernatural is above the natural and if you want to walk with God you have to walk by faith.

> *Now faith is the substance of things hoped for, the evidence of things not seen. For by it the elders obtained a good report. Through faith we understand that the worlds were framed by the word of God, so that things which are seen were not made of things which do appear.*
>
> —Hebrews 11:1-3

If you are going to operate in the realm of vision and prophecy, you have to walk by faith. You cannot walk by sight.

> *(For we walk by faith, not by sight:)*
>
> —2 Corinthians 5:7

Walking by sight means you attempt to base your life on the information you receive from the natural realm, where your five senses operate. It implies that you want to reason and understand everything you do and say. You will never function in the supernatural when you walk by sight and yield to the dictates of the flesh.

The prophetic anointing is a very powerful trans-generational anointing that functions under the influence of the inspiration of God. You prophesy when you are inspired by the Spirit of God.

But there is a spirit in man: and the inspiration of the Almighty giveth them understanding.
—Job 32:8

The inspiration of God is the breath of God. From the original translation, breath is translated Spirit. When you speak about the breath of God, you are speaking about the Spirit of God. One of the operations and manifestations of the Spirit of God is that He moves and inspires people to prophesy.

We have also a more sure word of prophecy; whereunto ye do well that ye take heed, as unto a light that shineth in a dark place, until the day dawn, and the day star arise in your hearts; Knowing this first, that no prophecy of the scripture is of any private interpretation.

For the prophecy came not in old time by the will of man: but holy men of God spake as they were moved by the Holy Ghost.
—2 Peter 1:19-21

In order to prophesy, you have to be moved by the Holy Ghost. You should be operating in the realm of the overflow anointing. When you give your life to Christ, the Holy Spirit comes to dwell in you and you experience the indwelling of the Holy Ghost. This is also known as the well stage of salvation. After that, there is another encounter you must experience: the infilling of the Holy Ghost. The infilling of the Holy Ghost is known as the river stage, which is also the realm of the overflow where the Holy Spirit is in absolute control of your life. At this stage He can guide, empower, and manifest through you to be a blessing to your generation and generations yet unborn.

> *In the last day, that great day of the feast, Jesus stood and cried, saying, If any man thirst, let him come unto me and drink. He that believeth on me, as the scripture hath said, out of his belly shall flow rivers of living water. (But this spake he of the Spirit, which they that believe on him should receive: for the Holy Ghost was not yet given; because that Jesus was not yet glorified.)*
>
> —John 7:37-39

When the hand of the Lord came upon Ezekiel the prophet, he was supernaturally transported by the Spirit of God into the realm of vision into a valley of dry bones. He was taken there because he had an assignment. It is important for you to understand that divine assignments require:

- Focus and concentration.

- Total surrender and obedience.

- Supernatural and strong faith.

- Flexibility and adaptability.

- The anointing to prophesy.

In the midst of the vision, God asked Ezekiel a number of questions then He began to give him commands to prophesy.

The hand of the Lord was upon me, and carried me out in the spirit of the Lord, and set me down in the midst of the valley which was full of bones,

And caused me to pass by them round about: and, behold, there were very many in the open valley; and, lo, they were very dry.

And he said unto me, Son of man, can these bones live? And I answered, O Lord God, thou knowest. Again he said unto me, Prophesy upon these bones, and say unto them, O ye dry bones, hear the word of the Lord. Thus saith the Lord God unto these bones; Behold, I will cause breath to enter into you, and ye shall live:

And I will lay sinews upon you, and will bring up flesh upon you, and cover you with skin, and put breath in you, and ye shall live, and ye shall know that I am the Lord.

So I prophesied as I was commanded: and as I prophesied, there was a noise, and behold a shaking, and the bones came together, bone to his bone. And when I beheld, lo, the sinews and the flesh came up upon them, and the skin covered them above: but there was no breath in them.

Then said he unto me, Prophesy unto the wind, prophesy, son of man, and say to the wind, Thus saith the Lord God; Come from the four winds, O breath, and breathe upon these slain, that they may live.

So I prophesied as he commanded me, and the breath came into them, and they lived, and stood up upon their feet, an exceeding great army. Then said he unto me, Son of man, these bones are the whole house of Israel: behold, they say, Our bones are dried, and our hope is lost: we are cut off our parts.

Therefore prophesy and say unto them, Thus saith the Lord God; Behold O my people, I will open your graves, and cause you to come up out of your graves, and bring you into the land of Israel.

And ye shall know that I am the Lord, when I have opened your graves, O my people, and brought you up out of your graves,

And shall put my spirit in you, and ye shall live, and I shall place you in your own land: then shall ye know that I the Lord have spoken it, and performed it, saith the Lord.
—Ezekiel 37:1-14

The vision of the valley of dry bones was a national assignment that the prophet Ezekiel had to carry out. The hand of the Lord supernaturally transported him by the Spirit of the Lord into the valley of dry bones, and in that realm he had to cooperate and collaborate with the anointing to fulfill this divine assignment.

The command to prophesy was not once. There were different stages and phases of prophesying and each stage and phase had particular demonstrations and manifestations that took place.

It is important for you to realize that in this current dynamic, ongoing move of God, focus, persistence, obedience, and supernatural faith is absolutely critical. You cannot allow yourself to be distracted by unimportant events and people. You cannot respond to things that God has not assigned you to. You have to be very careful. One of the main tools and instruments the enemy is using and will use against you is distractions.

Remember, focus produces concentration, and concentration produces acceleration, and acceleration produces momentum, and momentum causes multiple breakthroughs. The enemy will slow you down and derail your destiny if he is able to distract you and break your focus.

Prophetic intercession for individuals, families, organizations, churches, communities, cities, nations, and generations requires strong focus, persistence, and supernatural faith.

It is time for you to prophesy!

You need to prophesy under the inspiration of the Spirit of God. You need to be moved by the Holy Ghost and He will give you the relevant utterance for every assignment. You need to submit yourself to the spirit of prophecy and allow the Holy Ghost to use you to prophesy to the four winds of the earth to release the breath of God into situations in cities, nations, and generations.

God is counting on you! He is trusting that you will respond to His call and come into total surrender and obedience. He promised to pour His Spirit upon all flesh, and He has already done it.

And it shall come to pass afterward, that I will pour out my spirit upon all flesh; and your sons and your daughters shall prophesy, your old men shall dream dreams, your young men shall see visions:

And also upon the servants and upon the handmaids in those days will I pour out my spirit. And I will shew wonders in the heavens and in the earth, blood, and fire, and pillars of smoke.

The sun shall be turned into darkness, and the moon into blood, before the great and terrible day of the Lord come. And it shall come to pass, that whosoever shall call on the name of the Lord shall be delivered: for in mount Zion and in Jerusalem shall be deliverance, as the Lord hath said, and in the remnant whom the Lord shall call.

—Joel 2:28-32

It is time for you to respond to the desperate cry of the Holy Spirit in your generation and become a yielded and available vessel of honor to our Lord. This is the season of the fresh outpouring of the Spirit of God, and God is counting on you to prophesy His plans, purposes, and counsel into manifestation in the earth realm.

Live long and prosper! Fulfill your destiny in the mighty name of our Lord Jesus Christ. Amen.

If You're a Fan of This Book, Will You Help Me Spread the Word?

There are several ways you can help me get the word out about the message of this book...

- Post a 5-Star review on Amazon.

- Write about the book on your Facebook, Twitter, Instagram – any social media you regularly use!

- If you blog, consider referencing the book, or publishing an excerpt from the book with a link back to my website. You have my permission to do this as long as you provide proper credit and backlinks.

- Recommend the book to friends – word-of-mouth is still the most effective form of advertising.

- Purchase additional copies to give away as gifts.

The best way to connect with me is: Revbulla@gmail.com

About Bishop Senyo Bulla

Bishop Senyo Bulla was called into the kingdom of God at a tender age of 8 and he begun to preach the gospel in his teens and has over 30 years of tremendous global ministry experience which includes overseeing diverse congregations and ministries.

He is the founder of Apostolic Breakthrough International Ministries, a fast growing dynamic multicultural ministry with a strong apostolic and prophetic mandate of global evangelization, church planting and missions.

As the Apostle of Strategic Breakthroughs, he is a prayer general and a well sought out global conference speaker, revivalist and author who walks and operates in a strong apostolic and prophetic office with miracles, signs, wonders, healings and deliverance.

Global ministry is his vision and he accomplishes that through many social media handles and outlets and Strategic Breakthroughs, a television ministry on The Word Network that empowers millions to fulfill their prophetic destiny.

Enjoy These Other Books and Resources by Bishop Senyo Bulla

Breakthroughs
Dominion Over The Grasshopper Mentality

These are very exciting, pressure-packed times, but they are also defining moments that will determine the manifestation, or derailing, of your prophecy and destiny. You are caught in the midst of trans-generational battles that are being won or lost by the choices you make or do not make. Breakthroughs - Living in the Realm of Divine Possibilities is designed to equip you with relevant navigational skills to empower you to win every battle you are engaged in.

The Triple Anointing
The Power That Makes Ordinary Men Extraordinary

Every new level of the anointing lifted David into new levels of authority which were accompanied by new levels of tests and trials. He operated as priest, prophet and king - the triple anointing in different dimensions. The New Testament believer has access to the triple anointing and this anointing gives one the supernatural ability to function as a priest, prophet and king.

Releasing the Latter Rain

This book will give you a revelation on how to deal with a barren ground, the power of women, the causes of open and closed heavens, how to keep your heavens opened, the time of rain, prophetic actions, the purpose of the latter rain, physical, spiritual and financial rain and much more. There are different dimensions of rain and they all have to be released into your life for the manifestation of your prophetic destiny.

You can order these books from www.senyobulla.net.

NEED A SPEAKER FOR YOUR NEXT PROGRAM?

https://www.senyobulla.org/engagement-request

TUNE IN TO MY TELEVISION AND RADIO PROGRAMS

The Word Network
Saturdays @ 10:30 pm EST 7:30 pm PST

Praise 104.1 FM
Live on Sundays @ 7:00 am EST 4:00 am PST

Releasing the Latter Rain

This book will give you a revelation on how to deal with a barren ground, the power of women, the causes of open and closed heavens, how to keep your heavens opened, the time of rain, prophetic actions, the purpose of the latter rain, physical, spiritual and financial rain and much more. There are different dimensions of rain and they all have to be released into your life for the manifestation of your prophetic destiny.

You can order these books from www.senyobulla.net.

NEED A SPEAKER FOR YOUR NEXT PROGRAM?

https://www.senyobulla.org/engagement-request

TUNE IN TO MY TELEVISION AND RADIO PROGRAMS

The Word Network
Saturdays @ 10:30 pm EST 7:30 pm PST

Praise 104.1 FM
Live on Sundays @ 7:00 am EST 4:00 am PST

Enjoy These Other Books and Resources by Bishop Senyo Bulla

Breakthroughs!
Dominion Over The Grasshopper Mentality

These are very exciting, pressure-packed times, but they are also defining moments that will determine the manifestation, or derailing, of your prophecy and destiny. You are caught in the midst of trans-generational battles that are being won or lost by the choices you make or do not make. Breakthroughs - Living in the Realm of Divine Possibilities is designed to equip you with relevant navigational skills to empower you to win every battle you are engaged in.

The Triple Anointing
The Power That Makes Ordinary Men Extraordinary

Every new level of the anointing lifted David into new levels of authority which were accompanied by new levels of tests and trials. He operated as priest, prophet and king - the triple anointing in different dimensions. The New Testament believer has access to the triple anointing and this anointing gives one the supernatural ability to function as a priest, prophet and king.

About Bishop Senyo Bulla

Bishop Senyo Bulla was called into the kingdom of God at a tender age of 8 and he begun to preach the gospel in his teens and has over 30 years of tremendous global ministry experience which includes overseeing diverse congregations and ministries.

He is the founder of Apostolic Breakthrough International Ministries, a fast growing dynamic multicultural ministry with a strong apostolic and prophetic mandate of global evangelization, church planting and missions.

As the Apostle of Strategic Breakthroughs, he is a prayer general and a well sought out global conference speaker, revivalist and author who walks and operates in a strong apostolic and prophetic office with miracles, signs, wonders, healings and deliverance.

Global ministry is his vision and he accomplishes that through many social media handles and outlets and Strategic Breakthroughs, a television ministry on The Word Network that empowers millions to fulfill their prophetic destiny.

If You're a Fan of This Book, Will You Help Me Spread the Word?

There are several ways you can help me get the word out about the message of this book...

- Post a 5-Star review on Amazon.

- Write about the book on your Facebook, Twitter, Instagram – any social media you regularly use!

- If you blog, consider referencing the book, or publishing an excerpt from the book with a link back to my website. You have my permission to do this as long as you provide proper credit and backlinks.

- Recommend the book to friends – word-of-mouth is still the most effective form of advertising.

- Purchase additional copies to give away as gifts.

The best way to connect with me is: Revbulla@gmail.com

He raiseth up the poor out of the dust, and he lifteth up the beggar from the dunghill, to set them among princes, and to make them inherit the throne of glory: for the pillars of the earth are the Lord's, and he hath set the world upon them.

—1 Samuel 2:8

These are seasons of supernatural strategic placements of God and manifestations and demonstrations of magnificent power and glory through the operations of the hand of God and the Spirit of the Lord.

It is time for you to operate in a fresh glory, a fresh outpouring of the Spirit, and the power of God. It is time for you to function in new dimensions of the realm of fresh fire!

Live long and prosper! Fulfill your destiny!

The combination of the operations, manifestation, and demonstration of the Spirit of God in the life of Joseph was undeniable.

And Pharaoh said unto his servants, Can we find such a one as this is, a man in whom the Spirit of God is? And Pharaoh said unto Joseph, Forasmuch as God hath shewed thee all this, there is none so discreet and wise as thou art.

—Genesis 4: 8 9

A heathen king who served and worshiped many gods and had many magicians, enchanters, diviners, astrologers, and star gazers could not deny the operation and manifestation and demonstration of the Spirit of God, the Holy Spirit, in the life of a man.

This is your season of supernatural rain. I prophesy and declare over you the miracles and blessings of open heavens and a fresh outpouring of supernatural rain and financial rain over every dimension of your life.

I declare that you will never be found lacking in any dimension of the manifold grace of God. I declare an abundance and overflow of spiritual gifts, natural talents, divine opportunities, and amazing blessings in every dimension of your life and in every season of your prophetic destiny.

I prophesy and declare over you that you are recovering from all your loses. There is a new, fresh, unique, and peculiar anointing coming upon you for the restoration of mantles that will supernaturally lift, propel, and set you in the midst of princes.

The Restoration of Mantles

Pharaoh was blown away, amazed, flabbergasted, awestricken by the manifestation and the demonstration of the unique combination of spiritual gifts and natural talents in a man.

> *But we have this treasure in earthen vessels, that the excellency of the power may be of God, and not of us.*
>
> —2 Corinthians 4:7

Pharaoh had no choice but to move into operation. Joseph received a restoration of mantles.

- He lost the first mantle of the coat of many colors.
- He lost his second mantle as an overseer in Potiphar's house.
- The third mantle that Pharaoh gave him, that he never lost.

> *And Pharaoh said unto his servants, Can we find such a one as this is, a man in whom the Spirit of God is? And Pharaoh said unto Joseph, Forasmuch as God hath shewed thee all this, there is none so discreet and wise as thou art: Thou shalt be over my house, and according unto thy word shall all my people be ruled: only in the throne will I be greater than thou. And Pharaoh said unto Joseph, See, I have set thee over all the land of Egypt. And Pharaoh took off his ring from his hand, and put it upon Joseph's hand, and arrayed him in vestures of fine linen, and put a gold chain about his neck; And made him to ride in the second chariot which he had; and they cried before him, Bow the knee: and he made him ruler over all the land of Egypt.*
>
> —Genesis 41:38-43

He ended up in prison and met the baker and butler of Pharaoh. This too was a divine appointment, an appointment of destiny. Scripture does not reveal how long they were in prison before the baker and butler had their dreams and visions, but scripture reveals that after Joseph interpreted their dreams and visions, and his interpretation came to pass, the butler was restored, but for two full years he did not remember Joseph.

Divine appointments and the fulfillment of vision takes time. I don't know whether you have the patience and stamina to wait for the manifestation of vision for your financial destiny.

When Pharaoh dreamt, no one could interpret his dreams! Then the butler remembered Joseph.

Understand, despite how men treat you, God will still bring his counsel to pass. Understand His counsel is not about what men want or don't want, who or what they like or don't like. It is about the prophetic will and counsel of God!

God will use different men and different situations, circumstances, and events—the good, the bad, and the ugly—to bring His eternal purposes and counsel to pass.

Only Joseph had the unique and undeniable manifestation and demonstration of the unusual and peculiar spiritual gifts and natural talents needed to prophetically break down and interpret Pharaoh's dreams and visions.

whole staff of bread. He sent a man before them, even Joseph, who was sold for a servant: Whose feet they hurt with fetters: he was laid in iron: Until the time that his word came: the word of the Lord tried him. The king sent and loosed him; even the ruler of the people, and let him go free. He made him lord of his house, and ruler of all his substance: To bind his princes at his pleasure; and teach his senators wisdom.

—Psalm 105:8-22

Potiphar bought Joseph as a slave; then when he saw the Lord was with Joseph and everything Joseph did the Lord made it prosper, he promoted Joseph. He made him overseer over all his estate, domestically and internationally.

Potiphar covered the nakedness of the slave with special garments of prominence. Joseph came in naked as a slave, and God used Potiphar to cover his nakedness. The mantle he lost, the coat of many colors that gave him supernatural gifts and entrance into the realm of dreams and visions that was destroyed by his brothers was restored!

When Lady Potiphar set her eyes on Joseph she commanded him to sleep with her. After much torment and torture from Lady Potiphar, Joseph broke loose and tried to escape, but she caught his mantle as he ran out of the house naked.

When Potiphar came home, she lied and used the mantle she had taken from Joseph as evidence. This is where you see activities of false evidence, lies, misconstruing in the midst of scandals. Joseph lost his mantle once again!

You should read their stories, their pain, their tears, their domestic, financial, and political challenges. They dealt with various dimensions of contentions with the spirit of bareness in every generation, but the power of God through generational blessing and the activity of the sovereignty of God prevailed over all evil, and the counsel of God came to pass.

Joseph wore the coat of many colors and began to dream! He accessed the realm of the supernatural and logged into the visions of his great grandfather Abraham.

He was viciously attacked because of the mantle and its operations and activities. He lost the first mantle. He could not recover the loss of the first mantle. Then when he arrived in Egypt, Potiphar, Pharaoh's captain of the guard bought Joseph as a slave. Please understand all this was prophetic.

He hath remembered his covenant for ever, the word which he commanded to a thousand generations. Which covenant he made with Abraham, and his oath unto Isaac; And confirmed the same unto Jacob for a law, and to Israel for an everlasting covenant: Saying, Unto thee will I give the land of Canaan, the lot of your inheritance:

When they were but a few people in number, yea, very few, and strangers in it. When they went from one nation to another, from one kingdom to another people, He suffered no man to do them wrong: yea, he reproved kings for their sakes; Saying Touch not mine anointed, and do my prophets no harm. Moreover he called for a famine upon the land: he brake the to move and operate in the supernatural. The mantle gave him the power of vision.

Joseph lost the coat of many colors his father Jacob made for him through the hatred, envy, jealousy, and evil conspiracies of his brothers. It was the coat of many colors that gave him the abilty to be propelled into the realms of vision. He began to encounter the prophecies God had given to his great grandfather Abraham in the realm of the supernatural.

> *And he said unto Abram, Know of a surety that thy seed shall be a stranger in a land that is not theirs, and shall serve them; and they shall afflict them four hundred years;*
>
> *And also that nation, whom they shall serve, will I judge: and afterward shall they come out with great substance.*
>
> —Genesis 15:13-14

God Almighty was speaking to Abraham, His covenant friend and partner, in a vision about his seed. God was revealing His counsel to Abraham during apparent impossibility.

Abraham and Sarah were both old and they had no children, yet prophetically, God was revealing to Abraham in a vision about his seed, his child, and it came to pass. You must know that prophecy never fails!

Abraham gave birth to Isaac, and Isaac gave birth to Jacob, and Jacob gave birth to Joseph. It was easier said than done. There were generational curses contenting with all these patriarchs.

they cried before him, Bow the knee: and he made him ruler over all the land of Egypt.

—Genesis 4: 8 3

This is nothing but a supernatural manifestation and demonstration of God's power amid humanity. Vision for financial destiny is in its optimized demonstration.

Joseph as a young man received a coat of many colors from his father Jacob. The coat of many colors is a type of the ministry of the Holy Spirit and the manifestation of different dimensions of the anointing. Joseph operated under the influence of the triple anointing.

Prophetically, we live in the days of restoration of mantles. After the fall of man, Adam lost his garments and became naked and was driven out of the Garden of Eden, a place where the glory of God visited. Even before Adam was driven out of the Garden of Eden, God made new coats for him and his wife.

Unto Adam also and to his wife did the Lord God make coats of skins, and clothed them.

—Genesis 3 21

God was determined right in the beginning to show the enemy and all creation that He is a God of redemption and restoration. God is a special designer, a tailor who knows your measurements and will make new coats for you.

Right there in the garden you can see the operation of the restoration of mantles. This is because the mantle gave man the ability

CHAPTER FIFTEEN

THE RESTORATION OF MANTLES

Pharaoh made declarations over Joseph and Joseph entered into demonstrations of power and authority, and I declare in this season of supernatural strategic placements by the hand of God that this is your portion.

And Pharaoh said unto his servants, Can we find such a one as this is, a man in whom the Spirit of God is? And Pharaoh said unto Joseph, Forasmuch as God hath shewed thee all this, there is none so discreet and wise as thou art: Thou shalt be over my house, and according unto thy word shall all my people be ruled: only in the throne will I be greater than thou. And Pharaoh said unto Joseph, See, I have set thee over all the land of Egypt. And Pharaoh took off his ring from his hand, and put it upon Joseph's hand, and arrayed him in vestures of fine linen, and put a gold chain about his neck; And made him to ride in the second chariot which he had; and pour you out a blessing, that there shall not be room enough to receive it. And I will rebuke the devourer for your sakes, and he shall not destroy the fruits of your ground; neither shall your vine cast her fruit before her time in the field, saith the Lord of hosts. And all nations shall call you blessed: for ye shall be a delightsome land, saith the Lord of hosts.

—Malachi 3 7 12

The devourer is symbolic of anti-harvest forces. These forces are responsible for destroying your financial destiny. The season of the operation of every anti-harvest force against your financial destiny is over. In this new realm of vision for your financial destiny, you will walk and operate under different peculiar dimensions of the anointing.

All nations will call you blessed because there will be an evident manifestation of the power of the Holy Spirit in your life.

> *And if ye be Christ's, then are ye Abraham's seed, and heirs according to the promise.*
>
> —Galatians 3 29

You must possess your divine inheritance. You are an heir of God and a joint heir with Christ, and the Spirit of God, through the restoration of the mantle of glory, is bringing back to you everything you lost.

- You have been redeemed from every financial curse.
- You have been redeemed from every sickness and disease.
- You have been redeemed from every trouble and hardship.
- You have been redeemed from every satanic attack.
- You have been redeemed from sudden death and all the operations of the spirit of death.

Now it is time for you to walk in the blessings of your redemption; one of which is the promise of the Spirit. May a fresh outpouring of the Spirit of God that releases supernatural rain be upon you.

> **I prophesy and declare that your window of heaven is open, and God is pouring out upon you different dimensions of the rain of His blessing. He is rebuking the devourer for your sake.**

> *Bring ye all the tithes into the storehouse, that there may be meat in mine house, and prove me now herewith, saith the Lord of hosts, if I will not open you the windows of heaven, and*

And unto Adam he said, Because thou has hearkened unto the voice of thy wife, and hast eaten of the tree, of which I commanded thee, saying, Thou shalt not eat of it: cursed is the ground for thy sake; in sorrow shalt thou eat of it all the days of thy life; Thorns also and thistles shall it bring forth to thee; and thou shalt eat the herb of the field; In the sweat of thy face shalt thou eat bread, till thou return unto the ground; for out of it wast thou taken: for dust thou art, and unto dust shalt thou return.

—Genesis 3 17 19

The blessings and the power of redemption absolutely overrules and destroys this curse, and today I am here to enforce the absolute termination and destruction of any financial curse over your life through the blessings of redemption. According to Galatians chapter 3.

Christ hath redeemed us from the curse of the law, being made a curse for us: for it is written, Cursed is every one that hangeth on a tree: That the blessing of Abraham might come on the Gentiles through Jesus Christ; that we might receive the promise of the Spirit through faith.

—Galatians 3 13 14

It is time to enforce the powers of redemption over your financial destiny. You are the seed of Abraham because you are in Christ and you are an heir of God's covenant blessing. You cannot continue to walk in ignorance and allow the curse of the law to dominate your life.

- The blood that justified us.
- The blood that made us righteous.
- The blood that regenerated us.
- The blood that adopted us.
- The blood that made us a new creation.
- The blood that made us overcomers and gave us total victory.
- The blood that redeemed us from every curse and the hands of the enemy.

Beloved, the clothes God made for Adam and his wife represent the restoration of the glory of God. The lost garments of Adam were restored. The garments represent the mantle and the glory of God. It was the mantle that gave Adam the ability to function and operate in the realm of the supernatural.

The garments and the mantle represent the ministry of the Holy Spirit. The moment there is a restoration of the ministry of the Holy Spirit in your life, you have the supernatural ability to come back into the realm of vision for your financial destiny.

One of the main areas of life redemption prevails in is the area of finances. Remember that in the days of the fall of man, God in His absolute disgust pronounced many curses, and one of them had to do with the man.

conscience from dead works to serve the living God? And for this cause he is the mediator of the new testament, that by means of death, for the redemption of the transgressions that were under the first testament, they that are called might receive the promise of eternal inheritance.

—Hebrews 9 14 15

Christ hath redeemed us from the curse of the law, being made a curse for us: for it is written, Cursed is every one that hangeth on a tree. That the blessing of Abraham might come on the Gentiles through Jesus Christ; that we might receive the promise of the Spirit through faith.

—Galatians 3 13 14

This is where the benefits of redemption began. You have been redeemed from every curse. The Bible says:

Let the redeemed of the Lord say so, whom he hath redeemed from the hand of the enemy.

—Psalm 107 2

When the Lord God made coats for Adam and his wife, the blood in the skin of the coats represented the one and only perfect, spotless, and blameless blood of our Lord Jesus Christ. The blood without blemish or wrinkle!

- The blood that washed away our sins.

- The blood that purged and cleansed us from all sin.

- The blood that sanctified us.

CHAPTER FOURTEEN

THE BLESSINGS OF REDEMPTION

The good news is that God sacrificed an animal and covered their nakedness. He removed the fig leaves they had used to cover their nakedness, and He replaced it with the skin of an animal.

> *Unto Adam also and to his wife did the Lord God make coats of skins, and clothed them.*
>
> —Genesis 3:21

The sacrifice represents the one and only perfect sacrifice of the lamb of God that was slain before the foundation of the world.

> *And all that dwell upon the earth shall worship him, whose names are not written in the book of life of the Lamb slain from the foundation of the world.*
>
> —Revelation 13:8

> *How much more shall the blood of Christ, who through the eternal Spirit offered himself without spot to God, purge your*

Beloved, this is where curses began. I plead with you by the mercies of God, please stay away from anything that will activate curses and release the wrath of God upon you and the generations after you. This is where financial curses and the laws and cycles of hardship and difficulty began. Thorns and thistles represent laws and atmospheres of hardship and difficulties.

God didn't stop there. He drove Adam and his wife out of the garden. They were not just driven away from Eden, they were driven away from a realm. They were driven away from the realm of abundance, prosperity, creativity, productivity, fruitfulness, healing, peace, joy, dominion, and the supernatural. They were driven away from God's presence.

conception; in sorrow thou shalt bring forth children; and thy desire shall be to thy husband, and he shall rule over thee. And unto Adam he said, Because thou hast hearkened unto the voice of thy wife, and hast eaten of the tree, of which I commanded thee, saying, Thou shalt not eat of it: cursed is the ground for thy sake; in sorrow shalt thou eat of it all the days of thy life; Thorns also and thistles shall it bring forth to thee; and thou shalt eat of the herb of the field; In the sweat of thy face shalt thou eat bread, till thou return unto the ground; for out of it wast thou taken: for dust thou art, and unto dust shalt thou return.

—Genesis 3 14 19

This is where curses began. God was the first to curse! He was so hurt and disappointed when His plan for the human race was thwarted and messed up. He vented out His disgust, and He cursed.

- He cursed the serpent.

- He immobilized the serpent.

- He cursed the serpent and his seed and put them in a captivity.

- He cursed the woman.

- He cursed the man.

- He cursed the ground.

- He released the curse of death.

CHAPTER THIRTEEN

EXPOSING THE FOUNDATION OF CURSES

I know you will say this is strange. However, it is in the scriptures; that is why I included the scriptural reference right there, Malachi 3:8-9! God was so abused and disrespected that He began to curse His own children and demand for repentance!

In the beginning when man sinned against God, He cursed! Yes, He did.

> *And the Lord God said unto the serpent, Because thou hast done this, thou art cursed above all cattle, and above every beast of the field; upon thy belly shalt thou go, and dust shalt thou eat all the days of thy life: And I will put enmity between thee and the woman, and between thy seed and her seed; it shall bruise thy head, and thou shalt bruise his heel. Unto the woman he said, I will greatly multiply thy sorrow and thy*

God was so taken advantage of and abused that He began to call His own children robbers! I thought He would stop there, but He didn't. You know what He began to do? He began to curse!

Will a man rob God? Yet ye have robbed me. But ye say, Wherein have we robbed thee? In tithes and offerings. Ye are cursed with a curse: for ye have robbed me, even this whole nation.

—Malachi 3 8 9

them, fought for them, opened the heavens, gave them rain, blessed them, prospered them, and answered their prayers.

What did he get in return? Dishonor, disrespect, unfaithfulness, lying, dishonesty, and ingratitude. And this is a short list of the terrible treatment He received.

By the way, a tithe is 10 percent of your income (salary, wages, commissions, etc.). Ten percent of a thousand dollars is not fifty dollars! I thought I should make that clear because it seems that when the time comes to tithe, the calculator suddenly has problems. The battery doesn't work well, or the figures don't add correctly! Suddenly, 10 percent of ten thousand dollars becomes five hundred dollars. Because a thousand dollars, which is the right figure, is too much to give to God and His church! But we see nothing wrong with praying and begging God to give us a million-dollar deal!

I have seen Christians in desperate situations. I have prayed for many in my ministry who were in dangerously complicated situations. I have fasted and prayed for many of them that suffered with cancer, liver and kidney failures, issues with the pancreas, AIDS, and many other dangerous sicknesses.

After many days of prayer and fasting they get their breakthrough, whether it is a financial or healing breakthrough. The moment they receive their healing and deliverance they begin to be proud and misbehave and eventually leave the church or ministry.

> *Even from the days of your fathers ye are gone away from mine ordinances, and have not kept them. Return unto me, and I will return unto you, saith the Lord of hosts. But ye said, Wherein shall we return? Will a man rob God? Yet ye have robbed me. But ye say, Wherein have we robbed thee? In tithes and offerings. Ye are cursed with a curse: for ye have robbed me, even this whole nation. Bring ye all the tithes into the storehouse, that there may be meat in mine house, and prove me now herewith, saith the Lord of hosts, if I will not open you the windows of heaven, and pour you out a blessing, that there shall not be room enough to receive it. And I will rebuke the devourer for your sakes, and he shall not destroy the fruits of your ground; neither shall your vine cast her fruit before the time in the field, saith the Lord of hosts.*
>
> *And all nations shall call you blessed: for ye shall be a delightsome land, saith the Lord of hosts.*
>
> —Malachi 3 7 12

The subject of tithes and offerings have become very controversial in church circles. It doesn't have to be so because the scriptures are very clear on the issue. In the scriptures you just read, you discover that God, I mean the Most High God, is feeling abused and taken advantage of. If He had stopped there, with just expressing His feelings, it would have been okay, but He didn't stop there!

He felt abused by an entire nation and people. He had done so much for those who refused to honor Him and keep their covenant obligations. He had delivered them from their enemies, protected

CHAPTER TWELVE

TITHES AND OFFERINGS

Today there is a major crisis about offerings in churches. People have stopped going to church, and even if they go, they do not go regularly because of the offering!

I do not disregard the fact that people sometimes feel abused because of offerings in churches, but I also do not disregard the fact that people in church are sometimes carnal, selfish, and wicked. There must be a balance, and the balance is the guidance of the Spirit.

Whoever is receiving the offering must be led, guided, and controlled by the Spirit. In addition, whoever is giving the offering must have a willing and a generous heart and must also be led, guided, and controlled by the Spirit. Any extreme can be abusive in either direction.

God and His work can be abused, God will see the abuse and He will call His own people robbers and thieves.

that I shew thee, after the pattern of the tabernacle, and the pattern of all the instruments thereof, even so shall ye make it.
—Exodus 24:15-25:9

God spoke about offering.

"Offering?"

Yes, OFFERING!

details and patterns for the building of the tabernacle that would be a model for supernatural church growth and an international and global leadership manual.

Will you pass the first test? Can you sit still for six days and not fidget?

When God came out, the first thing He said on the seventh day was:

> *And Moses went up into the mount, and a cloud covered the mount. And the glory of the Lord abode upon mount Sinai, and the cloud covered it six days: and the seventh day he called unto Moses out of the midst of the cloud. And sight of the glory of the Lord was like devouring fire on the top of the mount in the eyes of the children of Israel. And Moses went into the midst of the cloud, and gat him up into the mount: and Moses was in the mount forty days and forty nights.*
>
> *And the Lord spake to Moses, saying, Speak unto the children of Israel, that they bring me an offering, of every man that giveth it willingly with his heart ye shall take my offering. And this is the offering which ye shall take of them; gold, and silver, and brass, And blue, and purple, and scarlet, and fine linen, and goats' hair, And rams' skins dyed red, and badgers' skins, and shittim wood, Oil for the light, spices for anointing oil, and for sweet incense, Onyx stones, and stones to be set in the ephod, and in the breastplate. And let them make me a sanctuary; that I may dwell among them. According to all*

vocating an irresponsible lifestyle of being only heavenly minded and not focused on caring for your earthly life, but too many of God's precious children are failing in the basics of divine encounters.

"Come up to me and be there" (Ex. 24:12). Has God been calling you to come to Him?

"When are You coming out?" Moses might have asked.

God didn't answer!

"How long should I wait?"

Again, no answer!

"Are You coming out soon?"

No answer!

Moses waited until the seventh day! God came out on the seventh day! And when He came out the first thing He spoke about, I honestly don't think you want to hear it…

OFFERING!

Beloved, when God comes out of His hiding place to reveal Himself to you in whatever form or fashion He chooses, He doesn't owe it to you to address and discuss what you want to hear. He will tell you what is on His mind and what His plans are.

God went into detail and gave very specific instructions. He told Moses He was going to give him tables of stone and instructions for him to teach; He didn't tell him that He was going to give Him vision, and purpose should be every Christian's priority. Is this where you are a miserable failure? If so, it is time for a change.

It is time to seek God, seek His presence, a divine encounter wholly, and you must start from humility and repentance.

Listen carefully, you can live and die and never fulfill the reason for your existence because you never passed the test of spiritual ascendancy. You never passed the spiritual mountain climbing experience to encounter the Most High God and receive the blue print for your life and destiny.

God is a master architect, and He has the blueprint for every dimension of your life and destiny. It is time to go to Him and spend some quality time with Him. It is time to make meeting with Him important. And don't hurry the experience or rush it.

This is a microwave, impatient, drive-through, pop in and quick stop generation. Unfortunately, you can't bring those bad attitudes and characters to God. Your busy schedule cannot be compared to His. How many children do you have? How many does He have? Who is more busy?

Beloved, pass this first test, don't fail to seek God and seek to encounter Him. You must make Him the most important aspect of your life, which is your spiritual life. Remember, you are initially a spirit. You have a soul (your mind, your will, and your emotions) and you live in a body.

Your body, the pressures of life, and all your other responsibilities are not more important than divine encounters. I am not ad-

First of all, when God called Moses to come up to him in the mount, He did not specify to Moses when He was going to reveal Himself or speak to Moses.

He just said to Moses, "Come up to me in the mount, and be there" (Ex. 24:12). This is where Saul and many others fail. They didn't have revelation of or the reverence needed for whom they were going to encounter, so they tried to do things on their own terms and not His.

Do you know who you want to encounter? He is the omnipotent, omnipresent, and omniscient God! The Creator of the universe, the galaxies, and all that can be found in them. He does as He pleases!

Do you have respect for who He is? He does not owe it to Moses or Saul, or you, or me to make an appointment. He doesn't call before He drops by to see anyone. He doesn't reveal when He will come out of His hiding place to visit you, see you, or talk to you.

"Come up to me and be there" (Ex. 24:12). I know you can't take it because you have a busy schedule. I know you can't take it because you deal with specifics. I know you can't take it because...the list goes on.

This is why some never come into divine encounters because they fail the first test. You may be successful in many endeavors of life, but when it comes to spiritual mountain climbing experiences you can be a miserable failure. Yet, seeking divine encounters should be the most important activity of your life. To have divine encounters and to come into the realms of divine revelation, *the glory of the Lord abode upon mount Sinai, and the cloud covered it six days: and the seventh day he called unto Moses out of the midst of the cloud. And sight of the glory of the Lord was like devouring fire on the top of the mount in the eyes of the children of Israel. And Moses went into the midst of the cloud, and gat him up into the mount: and Moses was in the mount forty days and forty nights. And the Lord spake to Moses, saying, Speak unto the children of Israel, that they bring me an offering: of every man that giveth it willingly with his heart ye shall take my offering. And this is the offering which ye shall take of them; gold, and silver, and brass, And blue, and purple, and scarlet, and fine linen, and goats' hair, And rams' skins dyed red, and badgers' skins, and shittim wood, Oil for the light, spices for anointing oil, and for sweet incense, Onyx stones, and stones to be set in the ephod, and in the breastplate. And let them make me a sanctuary; that I may dwell among them. According to all that I shew thee, after the pattern of the tabernacle, and the pattern of all the instruments thereof, even so shall ye make it.*

—Exodus 24 12-25 9

This is a powerful portion of scripture with many golden nuggets. It is a leadership and church building masterpiece. It is packed with revelation upon revelation. For the purpose of this study, we will pick only a few of them and come back another time for more.

CHAPTER ELEVEN

MOUNTAIN TOP ENCOUNTERS

When God wants to give you a vision or special instructions, He usually takes you into the realm of spiritual ascendancy. There are many who had special mountain top encounters that brought them into tremendous realms of vision and power and were subsequently used by God tremendously.

I want you to enjoy some of the experiences in scripture. Then it will be your turn.

> *And the Lord said unto Moses, Come up to me in the mount, and be there: and I will give thee tables of stone, and a law, and commandments which I have written; that thou mayest teach them. And Moses rose up, and his minister Joshua: and Moses went up into the mount of God. And he said unto the elders, Tarry ye here for us, until we come again unto you: and, behold, Aaron and Hur are with you: if any man have any matters to do, let him come unto them. And Moses went up into the mount, and a cloud covered the mount. And*

- Prayer or laziness and excuses?
- Spirituality or carnality?
- Bible reading or movies?
- Church activities or worldly activities and pleasure?

You have a choice to make! No one can force you in either direction. The choice is yours. You have to take into serious consideration that whichever way you go, there are consequences. Besides that, whatever you do, whatever you choose, you will stand before the judgment seat of Christ to give account of deeds done in the body.

For we must all appear before the judgment seat of Christ: that every one may receive the things done in his body, according to that he hath done, whether it be good or bad.
—2 Corinthians 5 10

Through Spirit-to-spirit connection, God expects you to respond appropriately to His dealings with you. If you respond appropriately to the dealings of God and you pursue the presence of God and continue in His presence, He will reveal Himself to you and bring you into divine encounters and visions.

You must be patient because God will show up in His time. He will not arrive on your schedule, but on His.

For the good that I would I do not: but the evil which I would not that I do. Now if I do that I would not, it is no more I that do it, but sin that dwelleth in me. I find then a law, that, when I would do good, evil is present with me. For I delight after the law of God after the inward man: But I see another law in my members, warring against my mind, and bringing me into captivity to the law of sin in my members. O wretched man that I am! who shall deliver me from the body of this death?

—Romans 7:19-24

The battle lines have been drawn:

- Between the inward man and the outward man.

- Between the Spirit and the flesh.

- Between sin and righteousness.

- Between good and evil.

- Between God and Satan.

- Between the old man and the new man.

- Between the world and the church.

You have to make a choice!

Who is going to get your time and attention?

- God or Satan?

- The Holy Spirit or evil spirits and demons?

- Righteousness or sin?

He waited a few minutes and the first bus he was on filled with passengers and left the station. He boarded the second bus, which took quite some time to depart. He was very late for his appointment, but he had peace in the second bus because he had obeyed the promptings of the Lord.

After about an hour on the second bus, they passed the first bus, which had been involved in a fatal road accident. Everyone on board the bus had died on the spot! Then the Lord said to him, "Do you see why, despite you being late for your appointment, I still commanded you to get off the bus?"

The precious man of God continued his trip praising and glorifying God for the strong promptings of the Holy Spirit that enabled him to escape the traps of sudden death.

Beloved, the promptings of the Spirit, the dealing of the Spirit, and the voice of God are absolutely important in every aspect of your life!

> **I pray for you today that God will enable you by His Spirit to be obedient to the dealings and leadings of the Spirit so you are not overtaken by the enemy. I pray your spiritual sensitivity and intuition will be heightened, and you will not operate in carnality and reasoning and miss the Spirit-to-spirit operations that can bring you deliverance and blessing that will enable you to fulfill your destiny.**
>
> **I pray for you today that you will not be ill-equipped in the battles of life against Leviathan in your office. The Leviathan in every aspect of your world.**

weight. What about your spiritual weight? How much do you weigh spiritually?

Are you a spiritual heavyweight or a spiritual lightweight? When you get into the boxing or wrestling ring with the enemy, who ends up crying? You or the enemy? Does the enemy win by a TKO (technical knockout) or do you win the fight? These are very important questions you need to answer because there are battles and storms of life and there is an enemy out there waiting for you.

Today, many of God's children are not armed and dangerous, nor equipped to fight against the adversary who is moving about as a roaring lion seeking whom he might devour.

There is a story about a man of God who was traveling for a very important appointment in a city about three hours by road from his home. He decided to take a bus to his early morning appointment there.

Unfortunately, he was running late for his appointment when he boarded the bus. Then, immediately he sat down in a seat, the Holy Spirit told him to get off the bus. Running late, he told the Lord, "Lord, I am already running late for this very important appointment, so if I get off the bus and take the next bus, I may miss the appointment." The Lord still insisted by the promptings of the Spirit for him to still get off the bus and take the next bus.

Since he was very acquainted with the voice of God and the dealings of God, although he was very late and was going to miss the appointment, he got off the bus.

> *But let it be the hidden man of the heart, in that which is not corruptible, even the ornament of a meek and quiet spirit, which is in the sight of God a great price.*
>
> —1 Peter 3 4
>
> *For which cause we faint not; but though our outward man perish, yet the inward man is renewed day by day.*
>
> —2 Corinthians 4 16

There is an inner man and there is an outer man. Most people focus all their attention on their outer man. They stand in the mirror to make sure that their outer man is looking good. They want to look good and acceptable to men, but what about looking good to God your Creator. When are you going to look into the spiritual mirror, the mirror of the Word of God, to see how you look spiritually to God?

> *But be ye doers of the word, and not hearers only, deceiving your own selves. For if any be a hearer of the word, and not a doer, he is like unto a man beholding his natural face in a glass: For he beholdeth himself, and goeth his way, and straightway forgetteth what manner of man he was. But whoso looketh into the perfect law of liberty, and continueth therein, he being not a forgetful hearer, but a doer of the work, this man shall be blessed in his deed.*
>
> —James 1:22-25

Today, the issues of weight and scales are major issues. There is a company named Weight Watchers and the people who join in stand on their scales a thousand times a day to check their body *with Christ; if so be that we suffer with him, that we may be also glorified together.*

—Romans 8:9-17

The Spirit bears witness with your spirit. You are a spirit and you were made in the image and likeness of God who is a Spirit.

When God wants to communicate with you, it is through a Spirit-to-spirit connection. These are the promptings, the leadings or dealings of the Spirit.

The Holy Spirit who is dwelling in you reaches out to your spirit and begins to prompt or urge your spirit in specific directions. When these promptings continue, the burden increases. If you respond appropriately you find yourself getting into spiritual activities of fasting, prayer, praise, worship, Bible reading or study. In all of these, God is trying to draw you closer to Himself.

If you do not respond appropriately, God will not continue forever, but the circumstances that will overtake you, may not be pleasant. Because you are a spirit and God's dealings with you will start through the operations of the Holy Spirit in your spirit.

And the very God of peace sanctify you wholly; and I pray God your whole spirit and soul and body be preserved blameless unto the coming of our Lord Jesus Christ.

—1 Thessalonians 5:23

communication. If you don't understand and accept that revelation, you will never place value and emphasis on spiritual things.

Know ye not that ye are the temple of God, and that the Spirit of God dwelleth in you?

—1 Corinthians 3 16

What? Know ye not that your body is the temple of the Holy Ghost which is in you, which ye have of God, and ye are not your own?

—1 Corinthians 6 19

But ye are not in the flesh, but in the Spirit, if so be that the Spirit of God dwell in you. Now if any man have not the Spirit of Christ, he is none of his. And if Christ be in you, the body is dead because of sin; but the Spirit is life because of righteousness. But if the Spirit of him that raised up Jesus from the dead dwell in you, he that raised up Christ from the dead shall also quicken your mortal bodies by his Spirit that dwelleth in you. Therefore, brethren, we are debtors, not to the flesh, to live after the flesh. For if ye live after the flesh, ye shall die: but if ye through the Spirit do mortify the deeds of the body, ye shall live. For as many as are led by the Spirit of God, they are the sons of God. For ye have not received the spirit of bondage again to fear, but ye have received the Spirit of adoption, whereby we cry, Abba, Father. The Spirit itself beareth witness with our spirit, that we are the children of God: And if children, then heirs; heirs of God, and joint-heirs

CHAPTER TEN

A SPIRIT-TO-SPIRIT CONNECTION

As we learned earlier, you are originally a spirit. You have a soul, and you live in a body. You were made in the image and likeness of God and God is a Spirit.

> *But the hour cometh, and now is, when the true worshippers shall worship the Father in spirit and in truth: for the Father seeketh such to worship him. God is a Spirit and they that worship him must worship him in spirit and in truth.*
>
> —John 4:23-24

God by nature is a spirit being, He is not a human. He is a being but not human. He lives in the spirit realm, and all His operations and activities originate from the spirit realm. When He wants to visit, speak, or reveal Himself to you, He does it spiritually.

It is Spirit-to-spirit! His Spirit, the Holy Spirit bears witness with your spirit. It is a Spirit-to-spirit contact, connection, and

ones to come down, O Lord. Let the heathen be wakened, and come up to the valley of Jehoshaphat: for there will I sit to judge all the heathen round about. Put ye in the sickle, for the harvest is ripe: come get you down; for the press is full, the fats overflow; for their wickedness is great. Multitudes, multitudes in the valley of decision: for the day of the Lord is near in the valley of decision.

—Joel 3:9-14

It is time to reap in the end-time harvest of souls into the kingdom of God. It is time to break the power of deception and the power of Leviathan over the souls of men and bring them into the kingdom of God. It is time for serious gospel ministry, time for global and personal evangelism for the lost to come into the kingdom.

Where are the mighty men and women of God who have a burden for the lost? Where are the apostles and missionaries of our time who can leave their comfort zones to aggressively advance this gospel of the kingdom to the ends of the world?

Too many are dying and going to hell because they will not leave their comfortable lifestyle to take this gospel into unreached territories of Christ. You are the man, you are the woman God is calling at this last hour in these end times to do whatever is possible to take the message to the lost.

Will you come under the influence of the laws of burden and arise and say, "Lord, here I am send me" (Isa. 6:8)?

the death. Therefore rejoice, ye heavens, and ye that dwell in them. Woe to the inhabiters of the earth and the sea! For the devil is come down unto you, having great wrath, because he knoweth that he hath but for a short time.

—Revelation 12:7 12

It is time for you to gain dominion over the dragon! I command you to declare war and prevail over the dragon and all his operations. You have dominion over Leviathan, that crooked and piercing serpent. The dragon in the sea of humanity. It doesn't matter what world you belong to, I command you to lift up a war cry against Leviathan, that wicked serpent and dragon that is determined to destroy our today.

Thou shalt tread upon the lion and the adder: the young lion and the dragon shalt thou trample under feet.

—Psalm 9: 13

Don't be ignorant and don't be a coward. Leviathan is on the move and he is the dragon in the sea of humanity. It is time to lift up a war cry against Leviathan and all his schemes and operations against this generation.

Where are the men and women of war? It is time to arise!

Proclaim ye this among the Gentiles, Prepare war, wake up the mighty men, let all the men of war draw near; let them come up: Beat your plowshares into swords, and your pruninghooks into spears: let the weak say, I am strong. Assemble yourselves, and come, all ye heathen, and gather yourselves together round about: thither cause thy mighty

- He is operating in the world of sports.
- He is operating in the religious and church world.

In other words, any other world you can think about, Leviathan, the crooked serpent, the piercing serpent, the dragon in the sea of humanity is in full and active motion.

He loves to operate behind the scenes, so if you don't have eyes to see him in the details, in the legalities, in technicalities, you pass by unable to recognize his presence because of his high levels of prudence, diplomacy, and sophistication.

In Genesis, he started off as the serpent in the Garden of Eden. By the time you reach the book of Isaiah, you discover Leviathan, the crooked and piercing serpent who has developed dragon like features. When you get to the book of Revelation, you discover a full-blown dragon.

And there was war in heaven: Michael and his angels fought against the dragon; and the dragon fought and his angels, And prevailed not; neither was their place found any more in heaven. And the great dragon was cast out, that old serpent, called the Devil, and Satan, which deceiveth the whole world: he was cast out into the earth, and his angels were cast out with him. And I heard a loud voice saying in heaven, Now is come salvation, and strength, and the kingdom of our God, and the power of his Christ: for the accuser of our brethren is cast down, which accused them before God day and night. And they overcame him by the blood of the Lamb, and by the word of their testimony; and they loved not their lives unto

- He is operating in the world of medical science, doctors, and nurses.
- He is operating in world of science and technology.
- He is operating in the world of business, trade, and commerce.
- He is operating in the world of finance and economics.
- He is operating in world of taxes.
- He is operating in the world of banking and accounting.
- He is operating in the world of education.
- He is operating in the world of information technology and computers.
- He is operating in the world of real estate, property and estate management, and wealth management.
- He is operating in world of transportation as people travel by land, water, or air. He is using terrorism and every evil mechanism to destroy.
- He is operating in the world of defense and security of nations.
- He is operating in the world of journalism and media aggressively.
- He is operating in the world of marketing and advertising.
- He is operating in the world of printing and publishing.
- He is operating in the world of fashion and beauty.
- He is operating in the world of music and entertainment.

Love not the world, neither the things that are in the world. If any man love the world, the love of the Father is not in him. For all that is in the world, the lust of the flesh, and the lust of the eyes, and the pride of life, is not of the Father, but is of the world. And the world passeth away, and the lust thereof: but he that doeth the will of God abideth for ever.

—1 John 2:15-17

Beloved, the lust of the flesh and the eyes. The desire for things of this world and the pride of life are still major, prominent, and strategic weapons the serpentine spirit still uses to derail the destiny of many. Be careful!

Today, he operates as a crooked serpent (corrupt). He is the piercing serpent, the dragon in the sea, he is in the sea of humanity. His name is Leviathan.

In that day the Lord with his sore and great and strong sword shall punish leviathan the piercing serpent, even leviathan that crooked serpent; and he shall slay the dragon that is in the sea.

—Isaiah 27:1

The serpentine spirit is still operating, scheming, and maneuvering in the sea of humanity. He is operating in all the world creating chaos and causing defiance toward God.

- He is operating in the world of politics.

- He is operating in the legal world of judges, attorneys, and lawyers.

I was naked, and I hid myself. And he said, Who told thee that thou wast naked? Hast thou eaten of the tree, whereof I commanded thee that thou shouldest not eat? And the man said, The woman whom thou gavest to be with me, she gave me of the tree, and I did eat. And the Lord God said unto the woman, What is this that thou hast done? And the woman said, The serpent beguiled me, and I did eat. And the Lord God said unto the serpent, Because thou hast done this, thou art cursed above all cattle, and above every beast of the field; upon thy belly shalt thou go; and dust shall thou eat all the days of thy life:

And I will put enmity between thee and the woman, and between thy seed and her seed; it shall bruise thy head, and thou shalt bruise his heel.

—Exodus 3 6 15

This passage of scripture is the sobering encounter of the fall of man. It clearly reveals the deception and the operations of the enemy. In the end, Satan, the devil, the deceiver was cursed. He is still in full operation today, using the same warfare, principles, and tactics.

By the way, he has upgraded and keeps improving on his arsenal, techniques, and battle strategies. He is more dangerous, subtle, and sophisticated than ever. If you are not vigilant to walk and operate in a deep sense of revelation, you will be outwitted and outsmarted by his masterful schemes.

CHAPTER NINE

THE OPERATIONS OF LEVIATHAN

When the enemy wants to attack you, he starts from outside inward. He lures, entices, seduces, tempts, and deceives you with things from the outside. Then he works his way to your heart.

> *And when the woman saw that the tree was good for food, and that it was pleasant to the eyes, and a tree to be desired to make one wise, she took of the fruit thereof, and did eat, and gave also to her husband with her; and he did eat. And the eyes of them both were opened, and they knew that they were naked; and they sewed fig leaves together, and made themselves aprons. And they heard the voice of the Lord God walking in the garden in the cool of the day: and Adam and his wife hid themselves from the presence of the Lord God amongst the trees of the garden. And the Lord God called unto Adam, and said unto him, Where art thou? And he said, I heard thy voice in the garden, and I was afraid, because*

for the Lord seeth not as man seeth; for man looketh on the outward appearance, but the Lord looketh on the heart.

—1 Samuel 16:7

Burden is the qualifying factor. The main and the only factor for responding to any call of God. God creates a restlessness and an agitation in your spirit that compels and drives you to seek God without reservation or excuses.

- Burden creates in you an attitude and lifestyle of endless selflessness and sacrifice like that of many of the missionaries and revivalists of old where you can say, "Lord, here I am. Send me."
- Burden drives you into unimaginable dimensions of prayer and intercession.
- Burden is the catalyst for revival and any move of God!

Today, many cannot respond to the call of God appropriately because they have not been through the full and complete process of burden, neither are they acquainted with the laws of burden.

This is the reason why revival has tarried; it is delayed because people do not accept a burden for the lost! They do not carry a burden for God and His kingdom. People respond to the call of God and enter ministry for all kinds of crazy reasons. You go into ministry or serve God because of burden, not for money, fame, popularity, ambition, pride, and an endless list of dead works.

Why are you in ministry? Why are you serving God in any capacity? If you are doing it to please people, then you are a man pleaser and you have already failed.

All the operations of God start from the inside; then He works His way out. When God wants to reach out to you, the first place He starts is your spirit or your heart.

But the Lord said unto Samuel, Look not on his countenance, or on the height of his stature; because I have refused him:

- Burden is a restlessness in your spirit that propels you into the presence of God.

- Burden is an agitation and dissatisfaction in your spirit that enables you to forsake everything that is fleshly and carnal so you can seek God.

- Burden creates an insatiable spiritual hunger and thirst.

- Burden compels you to abstain from food and every other form of pleasure and appetite to intensively seek God unapologetically.

- Burden delivers you from every form of distraction and brings you into a spiritual focus where you set your face like flint to pursue God aggressively until you find Him.

- Burden makes you a lover of God and the things of God.

- Burden puts you into a posture of worship where you humble yourself in deep reverence, submission, and total surrender.

- Burden gives you a servant's heart. It puts you in a condition where like Samuel you can say, "Speak Lord, thy servant heareth."

- Burden gives you a humility that cannot be produced through any other means.

- Burden gives you a broken heart and a contrite spirit.

Saul was afraid and his heart trembled greatly. He was literally traumatized, and the trauma and fear made him impatient, and he made rushed decisions that ended in defeat and destroyed his life.

You cannot be impatient when you seek God. You must approach God in humility and be patient as you wait upon Him. God does things in His time, and you must have the necessary reverence and respect for God to allow Him to reveal Himself to you when and how He chooses.

There is a realm of divine encounters, and only those with the fortitude and stamina required that are willing to pay the price and follow the laws of burden will access that realm.

When God wants to usher you into the realm of divine encounters, He begins by creating a sense of restlessness and dissatisfaction. The restlessness and dissatisfaction create a burden that compels and drives you to start seeking and inquiring for God.

The purpose of the restlessness and sense of dissatisfaction is to produce a burden. A burden that causes you to begin to embrace spiritual, mental, emotional, and sometimes even physical postures that enables you to access the realms of divine encounters.

The restlessness is an indication and a sign that you are not where you are supposed to be spiritually. You are not at the place or realm to receive divine encounters. You are not well positioned for a divine visitation, vision or to hear from God. Under those circumstances you become burdened.

CHAPTER EIGHT

THE LAWS OF BURDEN

When God wants your attention and He wants to visit you and communicate His plans and purposes to you, He starts by making you restless. The restlessness produces a burden and the burden makes you seek God.

Saul, the first king of Israel enquired of God but he lacked the necessary skills, stamina and fortitude that is required to come into the realm of vision and divine encounters. Read 1 Samuel 28 verses 4-7 again:

> *And the Philistines gathered themselves together, and came and pitched in Shunem: and Saul gathered all Israel together, and they pitched in Gilboa. And when Saul saw the host of the Philistines, he was afraid, and his heart greatly trembled. And when Saul enquired of the Lord, the Lord answered him not, neither by dreams, nor by Urim, nor by prophets. Then said Saul unto his servants, Seek me a woman that hath a familiar spirit, that I may go to her, and enquire of her. And his servants said to him, Behold, there is a woman that hath a familiar spirit in Endor.*

Your life will not be controlled by the dictates of men, situations, circumstances, or the devil. I declare that will not be your portion!

You will walk in dominion, and you will take charge!

Remember: The poorest person in the world is not the person who doesn't have money; the poorest person in the world is the person who doesn't have a God-given dream or vision, and is without a prophetic revelation.

The most frustrated person in the world is not the person confused about life events, but the person who has a dream or vision but does not know how to work it out, and who cannot make their dream or vision come to pass!

It is time for you to know what to do to come into the realm of divine encounters so that you can conceive and receive a God-given dream and vision that will transform your life and destiny and change you into the richest person in the world.

A dream or vision can give you everything you need. Your God-given dream or vision for your life will give you a purpose for living and a sense of direction.

The enemy has made sure that you live your life doing things you were not meant to do. You work jobs you were not meant to work. You live where you were not meant to live. You live beneath your level of dignity because you don't have a clear vision. There are people who live and die and never step into the real reason for their being.

You must be willing to pay the price for a God-given dream or vision. It doesn't matter how much it will cost you to get it, pay the price! Because a clear vision will make you all you were ordained by God to be.

> *He that walketh with wise men shall be wise: but a companion of fools shall be destroyed.*
>
> —Proverbs 13 20

Everyone cannot not be your friend, companion, or associate. Believing such is dangerous! There is an old phrase, "Show me your friend, and I will tell you your character." This is why parents have to be very concerned and keep an eye on who their children hang out with.

But the Bible says:

> *Iron sharpeneth iron; so a man sharpeneth the countenance of his friend.*
>
> —Proverbs 27 17

> *A friend loveth at all times, and a brother is born for adversity. A man void of understanding striketh hands and becometh surety in the presence of his friend.*
>
> —Proverbs 17 17 18

This verse describes the law of association and influence. A person who influences you has your ears. This is the first person you speak to on the phone when you get up in the morning, and they are the last person you speak to before you go to bed in the night. Who is your friend?

This person will determine the outcome of your destiny. They will determine whether you make wise or foolish decisions. They will determine whether you live or die! Who is your friend?

The treatments and cure for high blood pressure, chronic fatigue, stress, and many more medical situations are traced back to individual's sleep habits and patterns.

There are sleeping gadgets and machines people use to sleep at night; many can't go to bed without their sleeping machines!

But the Bible says:

> *It is vain for you to rise up early, to sit up late, to eat the bread of sorrows: for he giveth his beloved sleep.*
>
> —Psalm 127:2

According to the wise man and preacher, your sleep patterns determine whether you will be rich or poor. Discipline determines your sleep patterns and your levels of poverty or prosperity!

> *The slothful man saith, There is a lion in the way; a lion is in the streets. As the door turneth upon his hinges, so doth the slothful upon his bed. The slothful hideth his hand in his bossom; it grieveth him to bring it again to his mouth. The sluggard is wiser in his own conceit than seven men that can render a reason.*
>
> —Proverbs 26:13-16

When you don't have a God-given dream or vision, you settle for anything or everything. Anywhere or everywhere is your destination. Anyone or everyone is your friend or companion. That cannot be your lifestyle or the situation because the Bible says:

meetings. Lateness is a disease, and it can cost you everything in your life.

Discipline determines your reputation in life, it forms your identity. Discipline determines your level of integrity. People will chose how they either respect or disrespect you based on your level of integrity. They will track you, and they remember you by your discipline.

Without a God-given vision or dream driving and motivating you, you are the poorest person in the world!

Go to the ant, thou sluggard; consider her ways, and be wise: Which having no guide, overseer, or ruler, Provideth her meat in the summer, and gathereth her food in the harvest. How long wilt thou sleep, O sluggard? when wilt thou arise out of thy sleep? Yet a little sleep, a little slumber, a little folding of the hands to sleep. So shall thy poverty come as one that travelleth, and thy want as an armed man.

—Proverbs 6 6 11

Discipline will determine whether you sleep or not sleep. It will determine when you sleep, how you sleep and under what conditions you sleep. It will determine whether you eat before you sleep or not.

Today, the issue of sleep is a major issue and there are serious medical procedures about sleep. There is serious scientific research and studies done on sleep patterns to determine medical conditions.

Without boundaries, they are weak, they are lawless, rebellious, and without understanding. Know that there is an expensive price for a lawless life void of understanding. May this not be you or your loved ones portion.

> *I went by the field of the slothful, and by the vineyard of the man void of understanding; And, lo, it was all grown over with thorns, and nettles had covered the face thereof, and the stone wall thereof was broken down. Then I saw, and considered it well: I looked upon it, and received instruction. Yet a little sleep, a little slumber, a little folding of the hands to sleep. So shall thy poverty come as one that travelleth; and thy want as an armed man.*
> —Proverbs 24:30-34

Discipline is the master key! Discipline determines whether you succeed or fail. It determines when you eat, what you eat, how you eat, and whether you live or die. It determines whether you exercise and stay healthy or you live a reckless spiritual, physical, emotional, or financial life.

Discipline determines what you buy or you don't buy. It determines whether you use the credit card or not! It determines whether you live by the laws of delayed gratification or immediate satisfaction.

Discipline determines whether you pay your bills on time or not. It determines whether you are punctual for every appointment or are always late. A lack of discipline means you are late waking up, late for breakfast, late to the office, and late for board

> *godliness, faith, love, patience, meekness. Fight the good fight of faith; lay hold on eternal life, whereunto thou art also called, and hast professed a good profession before many witnesses.*
>
> —1 Timothy 6 10-12

The poorest person in the world is not the person whose bank account is in the red or is perpetually in overdraft. The poorest person in the world is not one who has taken out all kinds of loans and different lines of credit and cannot pay them off.

The poorest person in the world is not the person without food to eat or who has piles of unpaid bills and is struggling under the heavy load of financial stress. The poorest person in the world is the one who is without a dream or vision.

The Bible says:

> *Where there is no vision, the people perish: but he that keepeth the law, happy is he.*
>
> —Proverbs 29 18

When a child of God lacks a dream or vision, they live carelessly and walk aimlessly. They cast off all restraint because they lack clear direction in life. They have no discipline, guiding principles, rules, or regulations.

The dreamless and visionless will fight anyone who tries to help them by trying to put them on a schedule and bring discipline into their life. They are rude, disrespectful, and nasty without any apology.

CHAPTER SEVEN

THE POOREST PERSON IN THE WORLD

It is said that the poorest person in the world is not the person who doesn't have money. The poorest person in the world is the person who doesn't have a dream or vision. It is also said that the most frustrated person in the world is not the person confused about the events of life but the person with a dream or vision but who does not know how to work it out.

Emphasis should not be money, many of God's children have lost track and missed their destiny because all they think about is money. Money and the passion for money guides and controls their every decision and move.

The Bible says:

> *For the love of money is the root of all evil: which while some coveted after, they have erred from the faith, and pierced themselves through with many sorrows. But thou, O man of God, flee these things: and follow after righteousness,*

Fear thou not; for I am with thee: be not dismayed; for I am thy God: I will strengthen thee; yea, I will help thee; yea, I will uphold thee with the right hand of my righteousness.

—Isaiah 4: 10

For though we walk in the flesh, we do not war after the flesh: (For the weapons of our warfare are not carnal, but mighty through God to the pulling down of strongholds;) Casting down imaginations, and every high thing that exalteth itself against the knowledge of God, and bringing into captivity every thought to the obedience of Christ.

—2 Corinthians 10:3 5

God has only planned total victory for you. You cannot and will not fail.

was perfect in thy ways from the day that thou wast created, till iniquity was found in thee.

—Ezekiel 28:12-15

You must understand that this is where spiritual warfare begins. There is an enemy, and he is your adversary.

Be sober, be vigilant; because your adversary the devil, as a roaring lion, walketh about, seeking whom he may devour: Whom resist steadfast in the faith, knowing that the same afflictions are accomplished in your brethren that are in the world.

But the God of all grace, who hath called us unto his eternal glory by Christ Jesus, after that ye have suffered a while, make you perfect, stablish, strengthen, settle you.

—1 Peter 5:8-10

Remember, the devil is your adversary! As your adversary, your enemy and your opponent, his job is to attack, fight, resist and oppose you with adverse conditions known as adversities!

If thou faint in the day of adversity, thy strength is small.

—Proverbs 24:10

You cannot faint! You cannot give up! You cannot quit, quitters never win, and winners never quit! Don't say you are tired or that you can't take it anymore. You must continue to build up strength and fight. God Himself has promised to strengthen you and give you victory. Receive it!

- Troops that rule over states or regions.
- Troops that rule over cities and communities.
- Troops that rule over businesses, organizations, and churches.
- Troops that rule over families.
- Troops that rule over individual lives.

Sometimes I hear people insult Satan; they make comments like "Satan is foolish" or "Satan is stupid." That is completely wrong and far from the truth; he is very wise, intelligent, and well organized. He was created with wisdom and beauty, and when iniquity entered into him his wisdom and beauty were perverted.

> *Son of man, take up a lamentation upon the king of Tyrus, and say unto him, Thus saith the Lord God; Thou sealest up the sum, full of wisdom, and perfect in beauty.*
>
> *Thou hast been in Eden the garden of God; every precious stone was thy covering, the sardius, topaz, and the diamond, the beryl, the onyx, and the jasper, the sapphire, the emerald, and the carbuncle, and gold: the workmanship of thy tabrets and of thy pipes was prepared in thee in the day that thou was created.*
>
> *Thou art the anointed cherub that covereth; and I have set thee so: thou wast upon the holy mountain of God; thou has walked up and down in the midst of the stones of fire. Thou*

with him. And I heard a loud voice saying in heaven, Now is come salvation, and strength, and the kingdom of our God and the power of his Christ: for the accuser of our brethren is cast down, which accused them before God day and night. And they overcame him by the blood of the Lamb, and by the word of their testimony; and they loved not their lives unto the death. Therefore rejoice, ye heavens, and ye that dwell in them. Woe to the inhabitants of the earth and the sea! for the devil is come down unto you, having great wrath, because he knoweth that he hath but for a short time.

—Revelation 12:7-12

Satan, the devil, the accuser, has been cast down. He was cast down with a third of the angels. He used his tail to deceive a third of the stars of heaven, the angels of God. They are now known as fallen angels and they form Satan's hierarchy, his army and his troops.

For we wrestle not against flesh and blood, but against principalities, against powers, against the rulers of the darkness of this world, against spiritual wickedness in high places. Wherefore take unto you the whole armour of God, that ye may be able to withstand in the evil day, and having done all, to stand.

—Ephesians 6:12-13

Satan has:

- Troops that rule over continents.

- Troops that rule over countries or nations.

created. Thou art the anointed cherub that covereth; and I have set thee so: thou wast upon the holy mountain of God, thou hast walked up and down in the midst of the stones of fire. Thou wast perfect in thy ways from the day that thou wast created, till iniquity was found in thee. By the multitude of thy merchandise they have filled the midst of thee with violence, and thou has sinned: therefore I will cast thee as profane out of the mountain of God: and I will destroy thee, O covering cherub, from the midst of the stones of fire. Thine heart was lifted up because of thy beauty, thou hast corrupted this wisdom by reason of thy brightness: I will cast thee to the ground, I will lay thee before kings, that they may behold thee. Thou hast defiled thy sanctuaries by the multitude of thine iniquities, by the iniquity of thy traffick; therefore will I bring forth a fire from the midst of thee, it shall devour thee, and I will bring thee to ashes upon the earth in the sight of all them that behold thee.

All they that know thee among the people shall be astonished at thee: thou shalt be a terror, and never shalt thou be any more.

—Ezekiel 28 12-19

And there was war in heaven: Michael and his angels fought against the dragon; and the dragon fought and his angels, And prevailed not; neither was their place found any more in heaven. And the great dragon was cast out, that old serpent, called the Devil, and Satan, which deceiveth the whole world: he was cast out into the earth, and his angels were cast out

Then like Lucifer, there was a drastic shift. Saul moved from believing and following the principles of God to selfish pride, arrogance, egotism, stubbornness, and rebellion.

When Lucifer tried it, he was immediately cast out of heaven, and that is what happened to Saul. That is also what will happen to all who possess Luciferic demons and spirits.

> *How art thou fallen from heaven, O Lucifer, son of the morning! how art thou cut down to the ground, which didst weaken the nations! For thou has said in thine heart, I will ascend into the heaven, I will exalt my throne above the stars of God: I will sit also upon the mount of the congregation, in the sides of the north: I will ascend above the heights of the clouds; I will be like the most High. Yet thou shalt be brought down to hell, to the sides of the pit. They that see thee shall narrowly look upon thee, and consider thee, saying, Is this the man that made the earth to tremble, that did shake kingdoms; That made the world as a wilderness, and destroyed the cities thereof; that opened not the house of his prisoners?*
>
> —Isaiah 14:12-17

> *Son of man, take up a lamentation upon the king of Tyrus, and say unto him, Thus saith the Lord God; Thou sealest up the sum, full of wisdom, and perfect in beauty. Thou has been in Eden the garden of God; every precious stone was thy covering, the sardius, topaz, and the diamond, the beryl, the onyx, and the jasper, the sapphire, the emerald, and the carbuncle, and gold: the workmanship of thy tabrets and of thy pipes was prepared in thee in the day that thou was*

word of their testimony; and they loved not their lives unto the death.

—Revelation 12:10-11

Now they are not just on the team of the accuser of the brethren, accusing the brethren day and night before God; they are accusing Almighty God Himself saying He does not answer prayer. The devil is a liar; our God is a prayer-answering God. He is a miracle-working God! He is a mighty and faithful God!

O thou that hearest prayer, unto thee shall all flesh come.

—Psalm 6 2

When people refuse to apply the principles of God, and instead choose to do their own thing their own way, they cannot manipulate God to fulfill their agenda, they often say God doesn't answer prayers.

Nothing could be further from the truth. Too many prayers have been answered and too many miracles have been performed for us to sit down and allow a wicked and ungodly generation to falsely accuse our God.

Some of us are jealous for the name of the Lord because He has done beyond amazing, wondrous, mind-blowing, jaw-dropping miracles. We will not sit down and allow His name to be defiled by those who want to turn to witchcraft believing God doesn't answer prayers.

This is exactly what happened to Saul. He started off as God's chosen king; he enjoyed the anointing and the presence of God.

CHAPTER SIX

THE ACCUSER

Those who accuse God have joined the team of the accuser of the brethren. When people walk in legalism it is because they are operating in dimensions of witchcraft. They have:

- A suspicious mind and spirit.
- A critical mind and spirit.
- A judgmental mind and spirit.

Legalism, carnality, and immorality are major platforms of witchcraft. People are quick to condemn and pass judgment. They don't stop at just passing judgment on human beings. They proceed further and pass judgment on God Himself!

> *And I heard a loud voice saying in heaven, Now is come salvation, and strength, and the kingdom of our God, and the power of his Christ: for the accuser of our brethren is cast down, which accused them before our God day and night. And they overcame him by the blood of the Lamb, and by the*

unto to your children: how much more shall your heavenly Father give the Holy Spirit to them that ask him?

—Luke 11:9-13

In view of these promises of God, how dare anyone accuse God of unanswered prayer. In the light of all these promises of answered prayer, how dare anyone allow another to say that God doesn't answer prayers!

If you know someone who believes God doesn't answer or is slow to answer prayer, consider buying them this book, so they can read the truth of God's Word.

The prophet said:

And it shall come to pass, that before they call, I will answer; and while they are yet speaking, I will hear.

—Isaiah 6 24

Call unto me, and I will answer thee, and shew thee great and mighty things, which thou knowest not.

—Jeremiah 3 3

Jesus said:

And whatsoever ye shall ask in my name, that will I do, that the Father may be glorified in the Son. If ye shall ask any thing in my name, I will do it.

—John 14 13 14

And in that day ye shall ask me nothing. Verily, verily, I say unto you, Whatsoever ye shall ask the Father in my name, he will give it you. Hitherto have ye asked nothing in my name: ask, and ye shall receive, that your joy may be full.

—John 16 23 24

And I say unto you, Ask, and it shall be given you; seek, and ye shall find; knock, and it shall be opened unto you. For every one that asketh receiveth; and he that seeketh findeth; and to him that knocketh it shall be opened.

If a son shall ask bread of any of you that is a father, will he give him a stone? or if he ask a fish, will he for a fish give him a serpent? Or if he shall ask an egg, will he offer him a scorpion? If ye then, being evil, know how to give good gifts

God does answer prayers. The psalmist said:

> *I sought the Lord, and he heard me, and delivered me from all my fears.*
>
> —Psalm 34:4

> *This poor man cried, and the Lord heard him, and saved him out of all his troubles.*
>
> —Psalm 34:6

> *The angel of the Lord encampeth round about them that fear him, and delivereth them.*
>
> —Psalm 34:7

> *The eyes of the Lord are upon the righteous, and his ears are open unto their cry.*
>
> —Psalm 34:15

> *The righteous cry, and the Lord heareth, and delivereth them out of all their troubles.*
>
> —Psalm 34:17

> *Many are the afflictions of the righteous: but the Lord delivereth him out of them all.*
>
> —Psalm 34:19

> *He shall call upon me, and I will answer him: I will be with him in trouble; I will deliver him, and honour him.*
>
> —Psalm 91:15

Saul had been disobedient, stubborn, and rebellious. He had not gone through a genuine process of repentance and yet he desperately needed God and wanted an immediate answer from God. He was demanding an immediate divine intervention, and there was no response from God.

> *And when Saul enquired of the Lord, the Lord answered him not, neither by dreams, nor by Urim, nor by prophets. Then said Saul unto his servants, Seek me a woman that hath a familiar spirit, that I may go to her, and enquire of her. And his servants said to him, Behold, there is a woman that hath a familiar spirit at Endor.*
>
> —1 Samuel 28 6 7

Like Saul, this is a microwave generation. Many are impatient and lazy and they want everything "now." Let's get it clear. Saul did enquire of God. The restlessness he felt led to a burden, and the burden caused him to enquire of God. Saul, however, didn't carry through the full process of being burdened to achieve the desired result—God's answer.

What do you do when you desperately need an answer and there is no response from God? This is often a major issue of concern in this generation. Many in this generation believe God does not answer prayers. Many in this generation are impatient, ungodly, and disrespectful; they have no reverence for God or His ways.

and spiritual conditions are an indication that you are desperately in need of an encounter with the supernatural.

God allows this restlessness to produce in your spirit what is known as a burden. A burden is a spiritual condition of restlessness that compels you to seek God.

When Saul was afraid and his heart greatly trembled, the next thing he did was to enquire of the Lord. But when he enquired of God there was no answer. The pressure was on and he needed a quick answer from God about the situation. He couldn't wait!

He couldn't wait upon God, neither could he wait for God! He needed an immediate response.

I hope you are not in a similar situation. When you start seeking God for an issue, you want a now response because you are busy; you have a very hectic schedule. But it is important for you to know that God has a busier schedule than yours. He has many children who want and need his attention; some need Him more than you. Why should God leave His children who have been in extended periods of fasting and prayer for forty days and nights, twenty-one days and nights, to attend to you who cannot even fast from six in the morning to six in the evening? Yet you want God to drop everything He is doing and attend to the impatient you!

Besides having a schedule more intense and hectic than yours, if you have not satisfied all the spiritual principles and postures that allow for the visitations of God, He is not under any obligation to attend to you.

There are times in life when you can be confronted with very serious issues, challenges, and difficulties that literally threaten your very existence. If there is no divine intervention or miracle, you know you are either going to die or face shame and reproach that could be irreparable. It could be a sickness or disease and the doctor's report leaves you in a state of perplexity, confusion, fear, and depression. It could be a legal issue that leaves you traumatized.

You are traumatized when you go to bed and you have sleepless nights, and you are traumatized when you wake up! Your trauma becomes the first thought that grips you and keeps you in bed until you know that if you don't get out of bed, you will be late for every appointment. It could be a financial situation of multiple unpaid bills that leaves you stressed out thinking about the various embarrassments confronting you. It doesn't matter what it is; you are restless, sometimes afraid, and often depressed. You still have to maintain your cool when you meet people and nobody knows what you are dealing with.

Saul's story involves great spiritual truths that will empower you to go in the right direction; his story cautions you to stay away from any form of witchcraft or occult. Saul was so traumatized by the battles confronting him, scripture says that "he was afraid and his heart greatly trembled."

Have you ever been afraid like Saul was? That is restlessness! It's not just restlessness but it also leads to agitations, vexations and provocations. All these moods, states of mind or emotions,

CHAPTER FIVE

THE RESTLESSNESS

There is a state of restlessness, agitation, and discomfort that naturally occurs when you are faced with serious life battles. Sometimes there is no imminent sign of trouble or danger, but you still experience a restlessness in your spirit. Saul, the first king of Israel, went through restlessness and fear when he was confronted with a battle he did not know how to handle. Read 1 Samuel 28 verses 4-7 again:

> *And the Philistines gathered themselves together, and came and pitched in Shunem: and Saul gathered all Israel together, and they pitched in Gilboa. And when Saul saw the host of the Philistines, he was afraid, and his heart greatly trembled. And when Saul enquired of the Lord, the Lord answered him not, neither by dreams, nor by Urim nor by prophets.*
>
> *Then said Saul unto his servants, Seek me a woman that hath a familiar spirit, that I may go to her, and enquire of her. And his servants said to him, Behold, there is a woman that hath a familiar spirit in Endor.*

Your days of spiritual famine, where you run to-and-fro looking for a prophecy or a prophetic revelation, is over. Your days of not being able to access the supernatural through the ministry of the Holy Spirit, dreams or visions is over.

Your days of pursuing witchcraft and psychic hotlines, fortune tellers, palm readers, divination, sorcery, necromancy, black and white magic is over! It is time for you to begin a dynamic and vibrant relationship with God that will place you in the realm of continual guidance.

There is a supernatural realm that God has destined for you, and I declare that now is your season to access that realm and live in total victory and become a champion in all the battles of life.

he shall hear, that shall he speak: and he will shew you things to come.

—John 16 13

There is a truth about your life. Those are the plans and purposes of God for your life. The Holy Spirit was there with the Heavenly Father and Jesus when they were taking counsel about you before you became a clot of blood in your mother's womb, so He knows the counsel of God for your life, and He also knows every detail of your future.

If you need details about the future, the scriptures declare that "He will shew you things to come."

Saul wanted details about the outcome of the battle with the Philistines and he went down the route of witchcraft, and his bad spiritual condition worsened, and he died.

> **I declare that will not be your end. There is deliverance for you, and I declare that the power of God is coming upon you right now to bring you into new dimensions of deliverance from every mistake of the past and any legal right or ground the enemy has against your life.**

Saul's heavens were closed, he lived outside the realm of vision. God would not speak to him through dreams, visions, or the prophets. If you live in a realm of spiritual dryness and are operating under closed heavens, you need to break out of those limitations and confinements.

- Command all the calculations and projections of witchcraft on all satanic calendars to be deleted, aborted, and destroyed in the mighty name of Jesus.

- Command a full manifestation of all the plans and purpose of God for your life.

- Command an erection of divine calendars with prophetic timetables and divine agendas with specific kairos moments to manifest for you.

- Command a release of all your blessing, miracles, and breakthroughs with speed. Command that there will be no more delays in Jesus' mighty name.

- Command all your divine helpers and advertisers to be released through divine connections.

- Command the release of divine assistance and total deliverance for every dimension of your life.

Saul was frustrated and desperate that he could not access the supernatural realm through the right way in spite of all his efforts, so he went the wrong way.

I want to advise you not to use the wrong way. You need the Holy Spirit because He is your guide, helper, teacher, counselor, intercessor, legal aid, and assistant. He will guide you into all truth.

Howbeit when he, the Spirit of truth, is come, he will guide you into all truth: for he shall not speak of himself; but whatsoever perverse generation that is caught in the trap and the snares of different dimensions of witchcraft.

- Witchcraft in the church.
- Witchcraft over the church.
- Witchcraft over the season.
- Witchcraft over your marriage and children and grandchildren (domestic witchcraft).
- Witchcraft over your business and finances.
- Witchcraft over your opportunities, miracles, and breakthroughs.
- Witchcraft over your mission, assignment, purpose, and prophetic destiny.

Prayer Points

The only way to get rid of witchcraft is to command its presence and effects be eliminated. Pray the following points to help you break free from any occult operating in and over your life, family, church, and nation. Turn the following prayer points into your personal prayer and declaration.

- Command all the powers of witchcraft over any dimension of your life to backfire in the mighty name of Jesus Christ!
- Command all the intentions, manipulations, and scheming of witchcraft over any dimension of your life to be aborted.

and hath given it to a neighbour of thine, that is better than thou.

—1 Samuel 15 22-28

God had a generational grudge to settle with Amalek because of what they did to His covenant children when He brought them out of Egypt on the wings of eagles, out of the iron furnace. They were in route to the land of promise and Amalek attempted to sabotage Jehovah's purpose and agenda. When God gave Saul the assignment, He was still angry with Amalek. He had anointed Saul to execute His purposes for Him. Saul failing in his assignment, it was a serious issue with serious consequences in the days of Esther when Haman the Agagite became an instrument in the hands of the enemy to fight and destroy the Jews.

You have to understand: When God gives you an assignment, it is not a game. You must fulfill all your prophetic assignments with obedience, diligence, and aggressiveness. If you don't, your failure can be detrimental to future generations.

God refused to speak to Saul. God rejected him and took the kingdom out of his hands. In his frustration and inability to come into the realm of dreams, visions, and the supernatural to hear the voice of God, he resorted to witchcraft.

The encounter with a witch did not save or spare his life. Following after familiar spirits, divination, sorcery, necromancy, stargazing, horoscopes, or being an observer of times did not save his life. Saul still died! This story is a warning to this ungodly and *memorial in a book, and rehearse it in the ears of Joshua: for I will utterly put out the remembrance of Amalek from under heaven.*

And Moses built an altar, and called the name of it Jehovahnissi. For he said, Because the Lord hath sworn that the Lord will have war with Amalek from generation to generation.

—Exodus 17:8-16

That was the generational grudge God had to settle with Amalek, and he sent Saul the anointed king of Israel to fulfill that assignment and he failed miserably (1 Sam. 15:1-28).

And Samuel said, Hath the Lord as great delight in burnt offerings and sacrifices, as in obeying the voice of the Lord? Behold, to obey is better than sacrifice, and to hearken than the fat of rams. For rebellion is as the sin of witchcraft, and stubbornness is as iniquity and idolatry. Because thou has rejected the word of the Lord, he hath also rejected thee from being king. And Saul said unto Samuel, I have sinned: for I have transgressed the commandment of the Lord, and thy words: because I feared the people, and obeyed their voice. Now therefore I pray thee, pardon my sin, and turn again with me, that I may worship the Lord. And Samuel said unto Saul, I will not return with thee: for thou hast rejected the word of the Lord, and the Lord hath rejected thee from being king over Israel. And as Samuel turned to go away, he laid hold upon the skirt of his mantle, and it rent. And Samuel said unto him, The Lord hath rent the kingdom of Israel from thee this day,

God assigned Saul to fight a generational battle with Amalek for Him. Remember, Amalek attacked Israel as they were leaving Egypt, and God engaged in battle with them.

Moses climbed the mountain with the rod of God in his hands, and as long as Moses' hands were lifted, Joshua won the battle in the valley. When Moses got tired and his hands came down, Joshua and the fighting men were defeated.

Aaron and Hur gave Moses a stone to sit on while supporting his hands on both sides, and Israel prevailed against Amalek. After Amalek was defeated, God vowed to fight Amalek from generation to generation (Ex. 17:8-16).

> *Then came Amalek, and fought with Israel in Rephidim. And Moses said unto Joshua, Choose us out men, and go out, fight with Amalek: tomorrow I will stand on the top of the hill with the rod of God in mine hand.*
>
> *So Joshua did as Moses had said to him, and fought with Amalek: and Moses, Aaron, and Hur went up to the top of the hill. And it came to pass, when Moses held up his hand, that Israel prevailed: and when he let down his hand, Amalek prevailed. But Moses' hands were heavy; and they took a stone, and put it under him, and he sat thereon; and Aaron and Hur stayed up his hands, the one on the one side, and the other on the other side, and his hands were steady until the going down of the sun.*
>
> *And Joshua discomfited Amalek and his people with the edge of the sword. And the Lord said unto Moses, Write this for a*

CHAPTER FOUR

EXPOSING THE SOURCE OF WITCHCRAFT

It is important for you to follow the sequence of events that lead Saul into such difficulties. How did Saul get himself into such a difficult state of spiritual bankruptcy and a condition of no return? It was not just one event that led him there but it started with stubbornness, pride, disobedience and rebellion!

> *Because thou obeyedst not the voice of the Lord, nor executedst his fierce wrath upon Amalek, therefore hath the Lord done this thing unto thee this day. Moreover the Lord will also deliver Israel with thee into the hand of the Philistines: and tomorrow shalt thou and thy sons be with me: the Lord also shall deliver the host of Israel into the hand of the Philistines.*
> —1 Samuel 28:18-19

Are you resorting to abominations because God is not speaking to you either by dreams, visions, or ministry of the Holy Spirit? Be careful because the battles and pressures of life can push you down a path you never planned to get on. Saul was faced with battles and when he saw the enemy's forces, he was afraid.

There are different kinds of fear, different reasons for fear, but any one of them can take hold of you and encourage you to commit one of these abominations. Saul was afraid! He saw the host of the Philistines and when he enquired of God, God did not answer him by dreams, visions, Urim, or prophets.

Saul did everything he could to hear the voice of God and receive a prophetic word, but it was to no avail. He was in a very difficult place. His heavens were closed; he was in a spiritual famine, and God had departed from him.

You cannot afford to be in the condition that Saul the first king of Israel, the anointed of the Lord, ended in. It is dangerous and costly. Your purpose, mission, and assignment will be at stake. Your very life and prophetic destiny will be in jeopardy.

When thou art come into the land which the Lord thy God giveth thee, thou shalt not learn to do after the abominations of those nations.

There shalt not be found among you any one that maketh his son or his daughter to pass through the fire, or that useth divination, or an observer of times, or an enchanter, or a witch.

Or a charmer, or a consulter with familiar spirits, or a wizard, or a necromancer. For all that do these things are an abomination unto the Lord: and because of these abominations the Lord thy God doth drive them out from before thee.

Thou shalt be perfect with the Lord thy God. For these nations, which thou shalt possess, hearkened unto observers of times, and unto diviners: but as for thee, the Lord thy God hath not suffered thee so to do.

—Deuteronomy 18:9-14

Ignorance is not an excuse, so whether you did what you did knowingly or unknowingly, you will face the severe consequences of the judgment of God like Saul did. The only way out is confession and true repentance.

Saul the first king of Israel knew the law of God, and that is why he eradicated and thoroughly annihilated witchcraft and all its accompanying evil spiritual practices. Yet when he got into a very difficult spiritual situation because of spiritual dryness and its consequences, he resorted to the abominable.

boring and unexciting. Many of God's people have been disappointed and offended in churches; there are a million reasons why people do not go to church or follow Christ. I hope you are not one of them.

However, if you have been harmed by church in some way, know this: the failure of some churches does not give you or anyone else the right to follow the devil! Here are a few scriptures that may help you.

There is a way that seemeth right unto a man, but the end thereof are the ways of death.

—Proverbs 16 25

Enter ye in at the strait gate: for wide is the gate, and broad is the way, that leadeth to destruction, and many there be which go in thereat: Because strait is the gate, and narrow is the way, which leadeth unto life, and few there be that find it.

—Matthew 7 13 14

There are things that the Word of God lists out as an abomination to God but today many of them are practiced and because of ignorance of the scriptures or blatant stubbornness and disobedience, people believe they can get away with some practices.

I can absolutely guarantee that it will catch up with you somewhere and you will face the fatal consequences of the traps of witchcraft and all evil spiritual practices even if you pursued it out of mere curiosity.

Today, witchcraft has been modernized and glamorized and those into witchcraft are not even ashamed to openly declare they are witches, wizards, warlocks, grand wizards, and grand masters of the occult.

It is a blasphemous and spiritual bankrupt and cursed generation dealing with all kinds of legalization of abominations, and that is why we are constantly facing the fatal consequences of cursed grounds.

Saul was anointed! There was a time he had an intimate relationship with the Holy Spirit of God. The Spirit of God came upon him and used him for divine assignments, but something went wrong somewhere.

Today, many consult the dead and carry out abominably hideous and strange practices because of the strong craving for spiritual power and the ability to see into the spiritual realm. Today's generation is going down the wrong path, but so many people are on the same wrong route that many feel forced to consider these practices acceptable in the name of religious cohabitation!

I want to ask you: Are you now or have you ever carried out any of these strange practices? Have you read any of those books on witchcraft or magic? Have you ever been through any form of spiritual initiation?

If you answered "YES" then you certainly need deliverance!

Today, many people have stopped going to church, stopped reading the Bible, and stopped praying because they say it is *be with me: the Lord also shall deliver the host of Israel into the hand of the Philistines.*

Then Saul fell straightway all along on the earth, and was sore afraid, because of the words of Samuel: and there was no strength in him; for he had eaten no bread all the day, nor all the night.

—1 Samuel 28 1-20

This is an amazing story packed with golden nuggets for people from all walks of life. You are looking at a king of Israel now consulting a witch. Remember, you could not become a king if you were not anointed.

Then Samuel took a vial of oil, and poured it upon his head, and kissed him, and said, Is it not because the Lord hath anointed thee to be captain over his inheritance?

—1 Samuel 10:1

Once upon a time, Saul was anointed and was the chosen of the Lord! The question is this: How could an anointed king of Israel end up consulting a witch for divination, sorcery, and necromancy?

And I want to ask you: Are you into witchcraft, divination, sorcery or necromancy? Are you into tarot cards, Ouija boards, palm reading, psychic hotlines, black or white magic, spiritisms, white or black garment churches (occultic), incense fluoride water, holy baths, swallowing concoctions, carrying out rituals at the cemetery or grave sites, animal or human sacrifices, or any strange spiritual practice contrary to the Bible?

And when the woman saw Samuel, she cried with a loud voice: and the woman spake to Saul, saying, Why hast thou deceived me? for thou art Saul. And the king said unto her, Be not afraid: for what sawest thou? And the woman said unto Saul, I saw gods ascending out of the earth.

And he said unto her, What form is he of? And she said, An old man cometh up; and he is covered with a mantle. And Saul perceived that it was Samuel, and he stooped with his face to the ground, and bowed himself.

And Samuel said to Saul, Why hast thou disquieted me, to bring me up? and Saul answered, I am sore distressed; for the Philistines make war against me, and God is departed from me, and answereth me no more, neither by prophets, nor by dreams: therefore I have called thee, that thou mayest make known unto me what I shall do.

Then said Samuel, Wherefore then dost thou ask of me, seeing the Lord is departed from thee, and is become thine enemy? And the Lord hath done to him, as he spake by me: for the Lord hath rent the kingdom out of thine hand, and given it to thy neighbour, even to David:

Because thou obeyedst not the voice of the Lord, nor executedst his fierce wrath upon Amalek, therefore hath the Lord done this thing unto thee this day.

Moreover the Lord will also deliver Israel with thee into the hand of the Philistines: and to morrow shalt thou and thy sons away those that had familiar spirits, and the wizards, out of the land.

And the Philistines gathered themselves together, and came and pitched in Shunem: and Saul gathered all Israel together, and they pitched in Gilboa. And when Saul saw the host of the Philistines, he was afraid, and his heart greatly trembled.

And when Saul enquired of the Lord, the Lord answered him not, neither by dreams, nor by Urim, nor by prophets.

Then said Saul unto his servants, Seek me a woman that hath a familiar spirit, that I may go to her, and enquire of her. And his servants said unto him, Behold, there is a woman that hath a familiar spirit at Endor.

And Saul disguised himself, and put on other raiment, and he went, and two men with him, and they came to the woman by night: and he said, I pray thee, divine unto me by the familiar spirit, and bring me him up, whom I shall name unto thee.

And the woman said unto him, Behold, thou knowest what Saul hath done, how he hath cut off those that have familiar spirits, and the wizards, out of the land: wherefore then layest thou a snare for my life, to cause me to die?

And Saul sware to her by the Lord, saying, As the Lord liveth, there shall no punishment happen to thee for this thing. Then said the woman, Whom shall I bring up unto thee? And he said, Bring me up Samuel.

CHAPTER THREE

THE TRAPS AND SNARES OF WITCHCRAFT

Saul, Israel's first king, is a serious example of someone who found himself in a state of a spiritual famine. In the midst of national and international battles he wanted the word of the Lord, but the Lord would not speak to him.

> *And it came to pass in those days, that the Philistines gathered their armies together for warfare, to fight with Israel. And Achish said unto David, Know thou assuredly, that thou shalt go out with me to battle, thou and thy men.*
>
> *And David said to Achish, Surely thou shalt know what thy servant can do. And Achish said to David, Therefore will I make thee keeper of mine head forever.*
>
> *Now Samuel was dead, and all Israel had lamented him, and buried him in Ramah, even in his own city. And Saul had put*

You do not want to live under closed heavens, in a condition of spiritual famine. This is a miserable state and condition to live in. When there is a famine of the word of the Lord, it is a famine of the prophetic word, there is lack of direction and divine guidance. People walk about in a state of confusion, agitation, and vexation. Thus, the people are troubled and perplexed.

Today, many find themselves in this major generational crisis. I pray that as you continue this adventure of discovery, you will recover all the necessary tools and equipment needed to empower you to break out of spiritual famines. I pray that God will give you grace to access the realms of divine revelation that will break you out of spiritual captivity and bring you into tremendous breakthroughs of spiritual rejuvenation and reanimation that will lift you into new heights of your destiny.

And they shall wander from sea to sea, and from the north even to the east, they shall run to and fro to seek the word of the Lord, and shall not find it.

—Amos 8:11-12

These are the days we find ourselves in. Everybody is looking for a prophetic word, dream, or vision. People will go to any extreme to hear "THUS SAITH THE LORD." The famine the prophet is speaking about is very clear. It is not a famine of bread nor a thirst for water but of hearing the words of the Lord. This is a spiritual famine. Under conditions of spiritual famines:

- The heavens over the lives of individuals, families, churches, cities, and nations are closed.

- The heaven is as iron and the earth is as brass.

And I will break the pride of your power: and I will make your heaven as iron and your earth as brass.

—Leviticus 26:19

- God seems distant and unreachable.

- Prayers don't seem to break through or penetrate into the heavens.

- There are no divine encounters and prophetic revelations.

- Access into the realm of dreams and visions is impossible.

- There are no angelic or divine activities and manifestations.

Understand that the grounds were already cursed during Adam's life because of high treason and disobedience. Now through the action of Cain, the cursed ground was cursed again making it a double curse.

And unto Adam he said, Because thou hast hearkened unto the voice of thy wife, and hast eaten of the tree, of which I commanded thee, saying, Thou shalt not eat of it: cursed is the ground for thy sake; in sorrow shalt thou eat of it all the days of thy life;

Thorns also and thistles shall it bring forth to thee; and thou shalt eat of the herb of the field; In the sweat of thy face shalt thou eat bread, till thou return unto the ground, for out of it wast thou taken: for dust thou art, and unto dust shalt thou return.

—Genesis 3 17 19

In this generation cursed grounds, caused by gang violence, murders, drugs, various crimes, epidemics, natural and national disasters, terrorism, political upheavals, and uncontrollable mass demonstrations and riots, are now uninhabitable lands. These conditions of natural and national disasters cause people to either be evacuated by them or the people leave themselves.

When living conditions become extremely dangerous and uninhabitable, the word of the Lord is desperately needed.

Behold, the days come, saith the Lord God, that I will send a famine in the land, not a famine of bread, nor a thirst for water, but of hearing the words of the Lord:

become rebellious and uncontrollable. They resort to abominable lifestyles; they legalize abominations, and they practice what is contrary to the laws of God without shame. Under conditions like these, there is an outbreak of gang violence and ridiculous crimes become fashionable or a thing of the norm.

These conditions create a state of emergency, depression, violence, suicide, and murder. Within situations like these are various forms of addictions and satanic religions that provoke God to anger. When God gets angry, He curses the grounds.

Cursed Grounds

And Cain talked with Abel his brother: and it came to pass, when they were in the field, that Cain rose up against Abel his brother, and slew him.

And the Lord said unto Cain, Where is Abel thy brother? And he said, I know not: Am I my brother's keeper? And he said, What has thou done? the voice of thy brother's blood crieth unto me from the ground.

And now art thou cursed from the earth, which hath opened her mouth to receive thy brother's blood from thy hand; When thou tillest the ground, it shall not henceforth yield unto thee her strength; a fugitive and a vagabond shalt thou be in the earth.

And Cain said unto the Lord, My punishment is greater than I can bear.

—Genesis 4:8-13

another woman told her to bring her son for dinner. They grilled and ate her son that night! The next day when it was the turn of the other woman to bring her own son, she hid him. Words cannot describe the depths of evil and wickedness people can practice in the name of survival during national and global depressions and economic and financial crises and recessions.

A lack of financial rain causes extreme financial hardships that lead to financial stress, which has become a number one killer in this generation.

Spiritual Famine

When there is a lack of spiritual rain, then there is spiritual dryness. There are fatal consequences of spiritual dryness. Spiritual dryness attracts a lot of demonic activity and cursed grounds.

When the unclean spirit is gone out of a man, he walketh through dry places, seeking rest, and findeth none. Then he saith, I will return into my house from whence I came out; and when he is come, he findeth it empty, swept, and garnished.

Then goeth he, and taketh with himself seven other spirits more wicked than himself, and they enter in and dwell there: and the last state of that man is worse than the first. Even so shall it be also unto this wicked generation.

—Matthew 12:3 5

When there is a demonic invasion over a people or generation, the people refuse to hear and obey the Word of God; they refuse to go to church or have anything to do with the things of God. They *of silver, and the fourth part of a cab of dove's dung for five pieces of silver.*

And as the king of Israel was passing by upon the wall, there cried a woman unto him, saying, Help, my lord, O king. And he said, if the Lord do not help thee, whence shall I help thee? out of the banfloor, or out of the winepress?

And the king said unto her, What aileth thee? And she answered, This woman said unto me, Give thy son, that we may eat him today, and we will eat my son tomorrow.

So we boiled my son, and did eat him: and I said unto her on the next day, Give thy son, that we may eat him: and she hath hid her son.

And it came to pass, when the king, heard the words of the woman, that he rent his clothes; and he passed by upon the wall, and the people looked, and, behold, he had sackcloth within upon his flesh.

—2 Kings 6:25-30

The king of Israel was traumatized by a case that was presented to him in the midst of a national famine. There are issues that traumatize presidents, prime ministers, monarchies, senators, governors, and leaders at different levels.

The king of Israel was traumatized because a woman brought a dire situation to his attention. This is nothing but raw witchcraft. The woman had been dealt with so unscrupulously that she could not recover. During the financial, physical, and spiritual famine,

So besides them taking double money, there was other money! They were to take the double money they brought back from Egypt from the first trip.

> **I declare upon you the mysteries of the blessings of triple money! Receive it now in Jesus' mighty name. Wherever you are, say, "Triple money is my portion!"**

Can you imagine? During a serious financial crisis, Jacob had double money and triple money! The blessing of the Lord it maketh rich and He addeth no sorrow with it.

In the days of the patriarchs, you find that there were famines in every generation. Today, every generation faces its own kind of famine in various dimensions. In every generation, there are physical famines, financial famines, and spiritual famines. But in the midst of famines, these patriarchs came into tremendous breakthroughs of wealth!

Financial Famine

When there is a lack of financial rain, there are financial famines and there the spirits of hardship and difficulty in operation. In a financial famine, people find it hard to make ends meet. They live from paycheck to paycheck and exist in extreme cases of indebtedness with ridiculous interest rates that make them drown in debt beyond recovery. In the days of Elisha the prophet we have an example of a financial famine like this.

> *And there was a great famine in Samaria: and, behold, they besieged it, until an ass's head was sold for fourscore pieces*

global recession, and they had to travel internationally to get food. I want you to pay attention to verses 11 and 12 of Genesis 43.

And their father Israel said unto them, if it must be so now, do this; take of the best fruits in the land in your vessels, and carry down the man a present, a little balm, and a little honey, spices and myrrh, nuts, and almonds:

And take double money in your hand; and the money that was brought again in the mouth of your sacks, carry it again in your hand; peradventure it was an oversight.

—Genesis 43 11-12

Double Money

This is where you discover the secret of double money! Double money during famine? In the midst of a global financial crises, Jacob still had double money.

> **I prophesy upon you the blessings of double money. I declare that any curse or invisible barrier that has hindered you from the miracle of double money is broken and destroyed today! I declare that you and the generations after you have inherited prophetic blessings that have brought you into the miracle of double money!**

You know, I believe it was triple money! Triple money because Jacob said, "And take double money in your hand; and the money that was brought again in the mouth of your sacks, carry it again in your hand, peradventure it was an oversight" (Gen. 43:12)!

the blame for ever. For except we had lingered, surely now we had returned this second time.

And their father Israel said unto them, If it must be so now, do this: take of the best fruits of the land in your vessels and carry down the man a present, a little balm, and a little honey, spices, and myrrh, nuts, and almonds:

And take double money in your hand; and the money that was brought again in the mouth of your sacks, carry it again in your hand, peradventure it was an oversight:

Take also your brother, and arise, go again unto the man: And God Almighty give you mercy before the man, that he may send away your other brother, and Benjamin. If I be bereaved of my children, I am bereaved.

—Genesis 3 1-14

This is a very moving story of the plight of a father, a patriarch, Jacob, amidst the manifestation of destiny. He had lost his son Joseph, and now there were contentions over his last son Benjamin.

Both Joseph and Benjamin were children of Rachel. It is obvious Joseph did miss his father, but he had missed his younger brother more! I am sure he had missed the days they used to play their version of soccer, football, baseball, or basketball. It had been many years and he couldn't wait any longer.

You are looking at a very serious family meeting amid a grievous famine. The financial crisis was global! It was a season of

In the next generation, there was famine once again. Financial crisis and difficulties, but God was involved in it. This financial crisis was going to bring Joseph's dreams into manifestation.

And the famine was sore in the land. And it came to pass, when they had eaten up the corn which they had brought out of Egypt, their father said unto them, Go again, buy us a little food.

And Judah spake unto him, saying, The man did solemnly protest unto us, saying, Ye shall not see my face, except your brother be with you. If thou wilt send our brother with us, we will go down and buy thee food.

But if thou wilt not send him, we will not go down: for the man said unto us, Ye shall not see my face, except your brother be with you.

And Israel said, Wherefore dealt ye so ill with me, as to tell the man whether ye had yet a brother? And they said, The man asked us straitly of our state, and of our kindred, saying, Is your father yet alive? have ye another brother? and we told him according to the tenor of these words: could we certainly know that he would say, Bring your brother down?

And Judah said unto Israel his father, Send the lad with me, and we will arise and go; that we may live, and not die, both we, and thou, and also our little ones.

I will be surety for him; of my hand thou require him: if I bring him not unto thee, and set him before thee, then let me bear

The Bible tells us:

> *Then Isaac sowed in that land, and received in the same year an hundredfold: and the Lord blessed him. And the man waxed great, and went forward, and grew until he became very great: For he had possession of flocks, and possession of herds, and great store of servants; and the Philistines envied him.*
>
> —Genesis 26 12-14

Isaac sowed and he received a hundredfold. The Lord blessed him and he became great. Did you notice the progression? It started when he began to sow! He broke through until the Philistines envied him.

When they saw Isaac's possessions during famine, it was unbelievable. They knew God was with him. Look at what Abimelech the king of Gerar told Isaac.

> *And Abimelech said unto Isaac, Go from us; for thou art much mightier than we.*
>
> —Genesis 26 16

Isaac's blessing and his wealth and prosperity attracted envy. The envy was not enough! Now the king himself is confessing, "Go from us; for thou art much mightier than we"! Isaac's reported wealth was unbelievable!

I need to caution you sternly, there is a level of financial anointing that produces financial dominion that stirs up envy and contention! Be careful because this anointing is dangerous. You are seeing the manifestation in the life of Isaac, and I can see that anointing coming upon you. Receive it now!

waxed great, and went forward, and grew until he became very great: For he had possession of flocks, and possession of herds, and great store of servants: and the Philistines envied him.

—Genesis 26:1-4, 6, 12-14

In every generation there are famines, or financial crises and difficulties. The famine during Isaac's life was different from the one Abraham experienced, Isaac used the same principles and mindsets his father used, but God said no.

He was told not to go down into Egypt but to dwell in Gerar. Then Isaac was inspired by God to apply the laws of sowing and reaping, which are serious biblical laws for financial prosperity and financial dominion.

Today, many of God's children struggle with this biblical law of abundance and prosperity. This is a law that will never change. You must change; you must come into dimensions of divine revelation and apply the law. Then you can reap the benefits.

Remember:

While the earth remaineth, seedtime and harvest, and cold and heat, and summer and winter, and day and night shall not cease.

—Genesis 8:22

Isaac applied the biblical laws of sowing and reaping and came into tremendous wealth.

> **I prophesy that you are coming out of every financial crisis a millionaire! The power of God will orchestrate divine interventions during every trouble and bring you out very rich. This is your season for a supernatural transfer of wealth.**

And there was a famine in the land, beside the first famine that was in the days of Abraham. And Isaac went unto Abimelech king of the Philistines unto Gerar.

—Genesis 26 1

In the days of Isaac, he was also faced with a challenging famine. However, Isaac came out of famine more powerful and greater than when he entered it.

And there was a famine in the land, beside the first famine that was in the days of Abraham. And Isaac went unto Abimelech king of the Philistines unto Gerar.

And the Lord appeared unto him, and said, Go not down into Egypt; dwell in the land which I shall tell thee of: Sojourn in this land, and I will be with thee, and will bless thee; for unto thee, and unto thy seed, I will give all these countries, and I will perform the oath which I sware unto Abraham thy father; And I will make thy seed to multiply as the stars of heaven, and will give unto thy seed all these countries; and in thy seed shall all the nations of the earth be blessed;

And Isaac dwelt in the land of Gerar.

Then Isaac sowed in that land, and received in the same year an hundredfold: and the Lord blessed him. And the man there was a divine intervention that brought about a supernatural transfer of wealth.

> *The princes also of Pharaoh saw her, and commended her before Pharaoh: and the woman was taken to Pharaoh's house. And he entreated Abram well for her sake: and he had sheep, and oxen, and he asses, and menservants, and maidservants, and she asses, and camels. And the Lord plagued Pharaoh and his house with great plagues because of Sarai Abram's wife. And Pharaoh called Abram and said, What is this that thou hast done unto me? why didst thou not tell me that she was thy wife? Why saidst thou, She is my sister? so I might have taken her to me to wife: now therefore behold thy wife, take her, and go thy way. And Pharaoh commanded his men concerning him: and they sent him away, and his wife, and all that he had.*
>
> *And Abram went up out of Egypt, he and his wife, and all that he had, and Lot with him, into the south. And Abram was very rich in cattle, in silver, and in gold.*
>
> —Genesis 12:15-20, Genesis 13:1-2

There was famine in the land, but Abram came out very rich due to a supernatural transfer of wealth. Through trouble and a mighty demonstrations of divine intervention, Abram came out of crisis a millionaire!

Famines are seasons for supernatural transfer of wealth. Famines in the scriptures are symbolic of financial hardships, global recessions, and times of financial depressions. Famines are also generational.

A famine occurred during Abraham's life, and another one in the days of Isaac, and still another in Joseph's lifetime. The famine during Joseph's life was the catalyst that manifested the dreams and visions he experienced after he wore the coat of many colors that his father, Jacob, made for him.

Famines are seasons of supernatural transfer of wealth and the manifestation of vision and destiny. This is why the scripture says:

> *He shall deliver thee in six troubles; yea, in seven there shall no evil touch thee. In famine he shall redeem thee from death: and in war from the power of the sword.*
>
> *At destruction and famine thou shalt laugh: neither shalt thou be afraid of the beast of the field.*
>
> —Job 5 19 20, 22

You cannot laugh at famine and destruction if you don't have a revelation of the supernatural transfer of wealth. There is no crisis or stress as traumatizing and as tormenting as financial crisis. It puts you in a state of fear for financial reproach and financial embarrassment.

Abraham went down into Egypt because of the famine. In Egypt, he got into a lot of trouble, but I believe he prayed and

CHAPTER TWO

DIFFERENT DIMENSIONS OF FAMINE

A famine is an extreme shortage of food. It is a period of starvation and shortage usually caused by a lack of rain. When there is a lack of any dimension of rain the consequences are fatal.

Physical Famine

The lack of physical rain causes physical famines where conditions of living become uninhabitable, and people must migrate to different geographical locations to survive. Usually outbreaks of diseases and epidemics accompany physical famines.

> *And there was a famine in the land: and Abram went down into Egypt to sojourn there; for the famine was grievous in the land.*
>
> —Genesis 12:10

Deliverance ministry was in full power. There is record of women healed of evil spirits. Mary Magdalene was delivered from seven devils. Joanna the wife of Chuza, Herod's steward, helped provide for His ministry needs and was delivered of evil spirits as well. This lady's husband worked in the White House; he worked in Buckingham Palace, so to speak.

There is no record of what capacity he worked in, but we are told he was Herod's steward. He could have been a senator, or a governor or mayor. We have no details, but he worked in the highest office of the land, and he was clearly wealthy. His wife needed deliverance, and she received through Jesus' ministry.

These women and many others were financiers of the ministry of Jesus Christ. They had a revelation of ministry. They had substance; they had money, and they saw their giving to the ministry of Jesus Christ as ministry.

They may not have been able to preach, teach, or cast out devils, but they fulfilled their ministry. I pray for you today, that as you enjoy ministry and experience deliverance, prophecy, miracles, signs and wonders you will not wait to be asked to give of your substance. I pray you will have a revelation of being a financier of the gospel of Jesus Christ. The spiritual gifts in the life of Jesus Christ brought millions into the kingdom.

in her mansion and attended to all Paul's and his apostolic team's hotel needs in Macedonia.

Lydia constrained them! She begged them and forced them to receive the finances they needed for their stay in that region. She took care of accommodation, hotel bills, food, and entertainment. I mean she made sure that the apostolic team was well taken care.

May God send more Lydias in this generation who have kingdom revelation, Lydias who don't have to be begged or pressured to do the kingdom work. Lydia is an example of a millionaire who became a gospel financier.

And it came to pass afterward, that he went throughout every city and village, preaching and shewing the glad tidings of the kingdom of God: and the twelve were with him, And certain women, which had been healed of evil spirits and infirmities, Mary called Magdalene, out of whom went seven devils, And Joanna the wife of Chuza Herod's steward, and Susanna, and many others, which ministered to him of their substance.

—Luke 8 1-3

This is the ministry of the master Himself, our Lord Jesus Christ. Jesus Christ had both a mobile and resident ministry.

In the above scripture it is clear that Jesus' ministry was mobile, and He was not alone. The twelve were with Him, His apostolic team traveled from city to city as Jesus not only preached but revealed the glad tidings of the gospel. He healed the sick and worked miracles!

there is an abundance and an overflow of the grace of God and the manifestation of the Holy Spirit with supernatural demonstrations of the power of God and tremendous operations of spiritual gifts.

There are revivals and different dimensions of breakthroughs. It is time for you to enjoy the manifestation of supernatural rain. Every spiritual gift that is bestowed upon you is done for your profit.

But the manifestation of the Spirit is given to every man to profit withal.

—1 Corinthians 12:7

Amazingly the manifestation of one spiritual gift can turn your world right side up! It can bring cities and nations to Christ. The operations of spiritual gifts are desperately needed for revivals in cities and nations. The operations, manifestation, and demonstration of spiritual gifts resulting from supernatural rain can release millions of dollars into the kingdom of God.

And a certain woman named Lydia, a seller of purple, of the city of Thyatira, which worshipped God, heard us: whose heart the Lord opened that she attended unto the things which were spoken of Paul. And when she was baptized, and her household, she besought us, saying, If ye judge me to be faithful to the Lord, come into my house, and abide there. And she constrained us.

—Acts 16:14-15

Paul and his apostolic team preached the Word of God, through the ministry of the Word, the Lord opened Lydia's (a business woman) heart. When her heart was opened she started a business

> *Now when all the people were baptized, it came to pass, that Jesus also being baptized, and praying, the heaven was opened, And the Holy Ghost descended in a bodily shape like a dove upon him and a voice came from heaven, which said, Thou art my beloved Son; in thee I am well pleased.*
>
> —Luke 3 21-22

The people went to be baptized under the ministry of John the Baptist, but there is no record of anyone receiving the outpouring of the Spirit of God. Like today, people just go through the motions. It's religion and not revival because people are not desperate for God and the things of God.

In the case of Jesus Christ, it was different. He had a unique and undeniable encounter. The Holy Ghost descended in bodily shape as a dove upon Him, and a voice came out of heaven and said, "You are my Son, whom I love; with you I am well pleased" (Mark 1:11 NIV). When Jesus was baptized there was divine validation! Even before His public ministry began, Jesus Christ had the rain of the Spirit fall upon Him. He was guided and controlled by the Spirit of God. He could hear the voice of God and enjoy the presence of God. This is His testimony.

> *And he that sent me is with me: the Father hath not left me alone; for I do always those things that please him.*
>
> —John 8 29

Throughout His life and ministry, and even during His death and resurrection, the Holy Spirit was always with Jesus Christ in a powerful and unique way. When there is supernatural rain,

This means where there is no room, no opportunity or way, your gift can and will create room, opportunity, and make a way out of no way. Financial rain activates the overflow anointing that empowers you to recover all lost grounds in life and come into stupendous wealth!

Supernatural Rain

There is also a supernatural rain, which is an outpouring of the Spirit of God.

> *And it shall come to pass afterward, that I will pour out my spirit upon all flesh; and your sons and daughters shall prophesy, your old men shall dream dreams, you young men shall see visions: And also upon the servants and upon the handmaids in those days will I pour out my spirit. And I will shew wonders in the heavens and in the earth, blood, and fire, and pillars of smoke. The sun shall be turned into darkness, and the moon into blood, before the great and the terrible day of the Lord come. And it shall come to pass, that whosoever shall call on the name of the Lord shall be delivered: for in mount Zion and in Jerusalem shall be deliverance, as the Lord hath said, and in the remnant whom the Lord shall call.*
>
> —Joel 2:28-32

Supernatural rain is the fresh outpouring of the Spirit of God. This occurs under an atmosphere of open heavens. The prayer life of our Lord Jesus Christ gives us insight into the requirements for the miracle of open heavens and the outpouring of the Spirit of God.

When there is financial rain, there is abundance and prosperity. No lack, no poverty, no indebtedness, no shame or reproach. The rain is always released as a result of love for God and obedience to His covenant obligations.

Once the conditions are met, God in turn fulfills His part of the covenant by opening the heavens and releasing the rain. In this case it is financial rain, which is an overflow of different dimensions of empowerment.

There is an abundance of potential, gifts, talents, opportunities, favor, and atmosphere and condition relevant for limitless success and prosperity.

In spite of how challenging or difficult life might be, if you have the relevant knowledge, understanding, and wisdom, you will have navigational abilities to come out of every difficulty and misfortune.

A man's gift maketh room for him, and bringeth him before great men.

—Proverbs 18 16

Charis is the original word for gift, and it speaks about grace and grace brings into manifestation endowments from the supernatural realm. God is the source, the origin, the dispenser, and the distributer of grace. He releases and imparts spiritual gifts and natural talents. The wise man who wrote Proverbs, from years of experience, said, "Your gift will make room for you."

Financial Rain

Now it is time to understand the importance of rain in conjunction to a bountiful harvest. Financial rain is the empowerment of God to gain wealth that results from the blessing of God. Blessings speak about the act or words of approval and encouragement. An atmosphere of blessing is an atmosphere or environment that creates happiness and welfare. Financial rain exists in an atmosphere of abundance and prosperity!

> *The blessing of the Lord, it maketh rich, and he addeth no sorrow with it.*
>
> —Proverbs 10:22

> *Be glad then, ye children of Zion, and rejoice in the Lord your God: for he hath given you the former rain moderately, and he will cause to come down for you the rain, the former rain, and the latter rain in the first month. And the floors shall be full of wheat, and the vats shall overflow with wine and oil. And I will restore to you the years that the locust hath eaten, the cankerworm, and the caterpillar, and the palmerworm, my great army which I sent among you. And ye shall eat in plenty, and be satisfied, and praise the name of the Lord your God, that hath dealt wondrously with you: and my people shall never be ashamed. And ye shall know that I am in the midst of Israel, and that I am the Lord your God, and none else: and my people shall never be ashamed.*
>
> —Joel 2:23-27

He told them the promised land drank water of the rain of heaven. The demographics and the landscape of the land He was taking them into was completely different from the land of Egypt that He had brought them out of.

The children of Israel were caught between their past and future, just like you are caught between your past and your future. You have a great financial destiny ahead of you if and only if you embrace these proven principles of financial dominion.

Egypt was a flat land in which they could use sophisticated irrigational techniques and systems for farming. The promised land was a land of hills and valleys, and it drank water from the rain of heaven.

In the promised land rain was important. The former rain determined whether the seed planted would grow or not, and the latter rain determined whether the harvest would be bountiful or not. The former and the latter rains in their due seasons determined the harvest the people of God would reap, which determined their prosperity and sustained their posterity. Without rain, crops would fail and without food, the people of God would not survive.

As you continue in this discovery, I want you to be determined and committed, to break out of ignorance and come into new revelatory knowledge. This type of knowledge will usher you into the influence of a tremendous barrier-breaking anointing that will destroy all ancient invisible barriers, limitations and restrictions. It will supernaturally lift you into new heights of your financial destiny!

know" does not work continually. It is time to make a drastic, deliberate shift and embrace new dimensions of knowledge, understanding, and wisdom.

> *For the land, whither thou goest in to possess it, is not as the land of Egypt, from whence ye came out, where thou sowedst thy seed, and wateredst it with thy foot, as a garden of herbs:*
>
> *But the land, whither ye go to possess it, is a land of hills and valleys, and drinketh water of the rain of heaven: A land which the Lord thy God careth for: the eyes of the Lord thy God are always upon it, from the beginning of the year even unto the end of the year.*
>
> *And it shall come to pass, if ye shall hearken diligently unto my commandments which I command you this day, to love the Lord your God, and to serve him with all your heart and with all your soul,*
>
> *That I will give you the rain of your land in his due season, the first rain and the latter rain, that thou mayest gather in thy corn, and thy wine, and thine oil. And I will send grass in thy fields for thy cattle, that thou mayest eat and be full.*
>
> —Deuteronomy 11:10-15

The outpouring of physical rain was part of the covenant blessings that the Almighty God had with the children of Israel. God made it clear, that if they loved Him with all their heart and soul and they served Him then He would open the heavens and give them the rain of their land in due season (the former rain and the latter rain).

you walk in determines the sustenance of your posterity. Rain has generational effects.

In scripture, rain is symbolic of blessings. As you study the scriptures you will find that there are different dimensions of rain.

Physical Rain

The first dimension is physical rain, which determines whether the weather is wet or dry. Understand that when God was establishing His covenant with the children of Israel on their way to their promised land, He made it clear to them that the land of promise He was taking them into was not like Egypt, the land they were leaving behind. Sometimes past experiences and the resulting mentalities can cause a major hindrance to your future and destiny.

Egypt is symbolic of the world, the kingdom of darkness, worldly and carnal behaviors and attitudes. These behaviors and attitudes can influence every dimension and phase of your life. In addition, they will be the deciding factor that determines the altitudes you can access and ascend into!

You need attitudes that are governed by principles of good understanding because:

> *Good understanding giveth favour: but the way of transgressors is hard.*
>
> —Proverbs 13 15

You cannot repeatedly transgress, or disobey, spiritual and financial principles while offering excuses of ignorance. "I didn't

CHAPTER ONE

SUPERNATURAL RAIN

There are different seasons in a year, and when God Almighty entered into covenant with Noah, he made it clear that:

> *While the earth remaineth, seedtime and harvest, and cold and heat, and summer and winter, and day and night shall not cease.*
>
> —Genesis 8:22

You have to understand that the principles that produce a bountiful harvest are critical in every generation. Even though rain is not mentioned in the scripture above, you know that seed without rain is dangerous. The former rain is needed just before and after you plant your seed, and the latter rain is desperately needed before the harvest.

The timing and the quantity of the outpouring of the rain determines the magnitude of the harvest. The magnitude of the harvest determines the level of success, prosperity, and financial dominion you enter into. The levels of financial dominion and authority table and tremendous measures of financial anointing that will make an indelible impact and lasting impressions.

The harvest of souls must be won and brought into God's kingdom. Disciples must be turned into apostles, prophets, evangelists, pastors, and teachers. Multiple churches must be planted with speed, and the Apostolic Mandate must be fulfilled with intensity and aggressiveness.

For the above reasons, I will be ministering on supernatural rain, dimensions of famine, the operations of Leviathan, snares of witchcraft, mountaintop encounters, financial dominion, and more.

This is a season pregnant with the potential to optimize destiny released through prophecy. You must stay focused in this season, because you will be stretched to crucify the flesh. It's necessary to have an insatiable desire for God and spiritual things in order to access new dimensions for your financial destiny!

There is a world out there waiting for you. There is no one like you! You are unique and you are chosen, called, and anointed for such a time as this. Rise up and fulfill the mandate for financial dominion.

I will see you at the finish line!

Forever in His Presence,

Bishop Senyo Bulla

INTRODUCTION

Apostolic salutations with great joy and excitement because of the supernatural activities and operations of the hand of God in your favor!

We live in perilous, changing, and challenging times. However, these are prophetic times that require multifaceted spiritual and leadership skills that demonstrate relevance to this stress-filled and pressure packed generation.

I welcome you to *Kingdom Wealth,* another important supernatural message. This encounter is designed to equip and empower you to quickly ascend, prevail, and succeed in your financial destiny. To ascend into higher heights, you need new dimensions of divine revelation to supernaturally propel you into new dimensions of dominion over spiritual, physical, and financial famines.

This journey is intense! It will lift you to mountain top encounters that will develop inner tenacity and fortitude. These are prerequisite traits to reach the financial destiny ahead of you.

There are levels of financial vision, and it is time for you to shift into a new level of wealth that doesn't happen by chance!

To reach a higher level, you need measures without limits. Enough is enough of ordinariness and mediocrity! You need no-

TABLE OF CONTENTS

Introduction vii

Chapter 1: Supernatural Rain 1

Chapter 2: Dimensions of Famine 13

Chapter 3: The Traps and Snares of Witchcraft 29

Chapter 4: Exposing the Source of Witchcraft 37

Chapter 5: The Restlessness 45

Chapter 6: The Accuser 53

Chapter 7: The Poorest Person in the World 61

Chapter 8. The Laws of Burden 69

Chapter 9: The Operations of Leviathan 75

Chapter 10: The Spirit-to-Spirit Connection 83

Chapter 11: Mountain Top Encounters 91

Chapter 12: Tithes and Offerings 99

Chapter 13: Exposing the Foundation of Curses 103

Chapter 14: The Blessings of Redemption 107

Chapter 15: The Restoration of Mantles 113

DEDICATION

To the future and all who have sacrificed and selflessly given time and time again.

May God continue to increase the wealth of your precious time, resources, gifts, talents and money for the aggressive propagation of the flames of revival.

May your names perpetually be inscribed as a memorial in the books of remembrance in the archives of eternity for underwriting the financial burdens of revival. More than ever before, financial warriors are desperately needed to support the Kingdom. You have tirelessly stood in the gap to ensure the proliferation of the prophetic and the fulfillment of destiny. May The Lord God El-Ha-Gibbor, our conquering King and Messiah, our champion and hero fight all your battles, giving you total victory and dominion from generation to generation in the mighty name of our Lord Jesus Christ.

Kingdom Wealth

Copyright ©2021 Bishop Senyo Bulla

All rights reserved. No part of this publication may be reproduced, distributed or transmitted in any form or by any means, including photocopying, recording, or other electronic or mechanical methods, without the prior written permission of the publisher, except in the case of brief quotations embodied in critical reviews and certain other noncommercial uses permitted by copyright law.

Unless otherwise indicated, Scriptures are taken from the KING JAMES VERSION (KJV), public domain.

Published by: HigherLife Publishing & Marketing
  PO Box 623307
  Oviedo, FL 32762
  AHigherLife.com

ISBN: 978-1-954533-63-9 (Paperback)
ISBN: 978-1-954533-64-6 (Ebook)

Printed in the United States of America.

10 9 8 7 6 5 4 3 2 1

KINGDOM WEALTH

KEYS TO ACCESSING YOUR FINANCIAL DESTINY

BISHOP SENYO BULLA

www.ingramcontent.com/pod-product-compliance
Lightning Source LLC
Chambersburg PA
CBHW070349240426
43671CB00013BA/2450